Mark Bouris has been involved in the finance and property sectors for over 25 years. He is Chairman of Wizard Home Loans, the Australian Financial Investments Group and financial services company Yellow Brick Road Group. In 2004 he was appointed Adjunct Professor (Banking and Finance, and Business Law and Tax) at the University of New South Wales, and he is an industry leader on consumer protection issues.

THE YELLOW|BRICK|ROAD TO YOUR FINANCIAL SECURITY

MARK BOURIS

ARENA
ALLEN&UNWIN

First published in 2008

Arena Books, an imprint of
Allen & Unwin
83 Alexander Street
Crows Nest NSW 2065
Australia
Phone: (61 2) 8425 0100
Fax: (61 2) 9906 2218
Email: info@allenandunwin.com
Web: www.allenandunwin.com

National Library of Australia
Cataloguing-in-Publication entry:

Bouris, Mark.
The yellow brick road to your financial security.

ISBN 978 1 74175 421 6 (pbk.)

Includes index.

Retirement—Australia—Planning. Retirement income—Australia—Planning. Investments. Retirees—Australia—Finance, Personal.

332.024014

Index by Russell Brooks
Set in 12.5/16 pt Bembo by Midland Typesetters, Australia
10 9 8 7 6 5 4 3 2 1

To my children,
WORK: it keeps the mind occupied and nimble and delivers purpose.
PLAY: it balances the time, effort and anguish of work.
FIGHT: only for what is worth fighting for.
LOVE: only what is worth loving, and do so with all your heart.
BELIEVE: in something, but believe every day.

CONTENTS

ACKNOWLEDGEMENTS

I'd like to thank the many people who helped me write this book. In particular I would like to show my appreciation to Mark Abernethy who spent many hours talking about this book, and writing many of the words that appear on the pages.

I'd like to thank Professor Ron Penny, from Good Health Solutions, for all his advice and good sense about diet, exercise, stress management and mental health. Similarly I appreciate Dr Jennifer Hunter's words of wisdom, and her continued support. She understands.

Finally, I'd like to thank Beverly Houterman from Yellow Brick Road for fact checking the book, and Sean Aylmer, also from Yellow Brick Road, for his help editing the book.

Thanks Mum and Dad, as usual.

INTRODUCTION: THINKING ABOUT THE FUTURE

There are two great dreams for most Australians: owning their own home and having a comfortable retirement. These two dreams form the bookends of many Australians' true financial focus. It's what keeps them working.

With your own house, you have a place to live, you have an appreciating asset and you have an asset against which you can borrow money to create more wealth. You may spend your whole working life paying off a mortgage, but you do it for good reason.

Then comes the comfortable retirement: this is the reward for all the hard work, including all the scrimping and saving over the time it took to buy the house. A comfortable retirement includes a house or apartment you can live in, but it also includes a source of income you can live on. You want the comfy nest, but you also need a food supply—which for most people comes via superannuation, shares, rental property or the pension. And in the case of retirement, you need a supply that lasts for the rest of your life.

It won't be enough

Australians love their homes. I started realising a few years ago that many Australians are well aware of the need to buy their own home and to pay it off by the time they retire. It makes sense because of having somewhere to live *and* earning money as the home gains value. And we're good at home ownership: we not only have one of the highest rates of home ownership in the world, but we also have among the lowest rates of mortgage default. Australia's home ownership rate is around 70 per cent of all households, the highest rate in the G7 countries except Italy, and the highest home ownership rate in the English-speaking countries, such as the United States, Canada, New Zealand and Britain. Housing is solid and it's useful, and that's why Australians like it so much as both an investment and as a haven for the family.

But having got the first imperative into their heads, Australians have not been so good at saving money for retirement. Why? Perhaps it's because we're optimistic people, so we don't look too far into the future, we don't expect to stop earning, and we don't think the good times will ever stop.

The AMP-NATSEM Income and Wealth Report (May 2002) spells this out. Looking at Australians aged 50 to 64, the report found that on average this age group was quite well off, with accumulated wealth of $240,000 per person. But the sting was that these people had most of their wealth in the family home. It wasn't income—it was equity. It was the value of their home minus anything they owed on it.

The average amount of retirement savings they could access quickly was $56,000. That provides for income per week in retirement of just $100.

In October 2006 the NATSEM organisation (National Centre for Social and Economic Modelling) came out with even scarier figures: half of Australian women aged 45 to 60 had $8000 or less in super and half of all males in the same age bracket had $30,700 or less in super. Most financial planners suggest a person needs about $30,000 *per year* in retirement to be comfortable. For couples, that figure is around $45,000 per year, according to the Association of Superannuation Funds of Australia (ASFA). And that's in today's dollars.

The age pension provides $13,000; the remaining $17,000 (or $32,000 for a couple) per year needs to come from superannuation or other investments.

It's a big problem and it will only get bigger. The number of people facing a shortfall will surge when the baby boomers start retiring. In May 2007 the federal government released its second Intergenerational Report, which looks at the implications of population changes on economic growth. It projected that by 2047 Australia's population would be 28.5 million and that one in four people would be older than 65—almost double the current level. The proportion aged over 85 will almost triple to 5.6 per cent of the population. Another way of thinking about it is to consider the ratio of workers to retirees. At the moment, there are five people of working age to support every person aged over 65. By 2047 there will be only 2.4 people of working age to support every person over 65.

The challenges are clear: people haven't saved enough for retirement and the problem will only get bigger as the baby boomers retire.

It's increasingly going to be one of the major regrets for generations of retirees: they didn't save more, didn't use the tax-effective superannuation system to provide for their non-earning years. When others were putting away for a rainy day, they were pretending the rain would never come.

And what of the age pension? Australia won't be able to afford to look after its retirees. We can't expect the next generation to pay much higher tax rates to fund the retirement of the current generation of workers. The age pension is either on the way out for all except the most needy, or it's going to be run down so much that middle-class people expecting to live to a certain standard when they retire won't be able to rely on the pension to do so.

We know these things. We know we have to have a home by the time we retire, and we know we have to save enough so we can enjoy our retirement years—years that will be extended given the high and rising life expectancy of what is, after all, a very lucky country. And we know that Australians are not saving enough for retirement.

But what do we do? Who do we turn to? Who has the

information we need to show us where we're going and how to get there? Is there a solution?

My story

In the last two years I've been on my own journey, on which I had to answer these questions for myself.

I had property, which I'd been buying since my twenties. And my partners and I had built a good property development business. But after we'd built Wizard Home Loans to a certain size, and sold it to the US company GE, I owned a lot of shares: I'd taken the entire purchase price of my portion of Wizard in GE stock.

This was a very exciting and successful time in my life but it was also a crossroads which brought me into contact with the issues I've mentioned.

First, I was at an age—49—when I had to be serious about saving for retirement. I have four sons and a number of business interests and I had to start thinking about the practicalities of retiring and how best to finance that. I hate to admit it, but I'd never thought about it before.

Second, when I sold Wizard and took all of my proceeds in GE stock, I was now in a high-risk position—I wasn't diversified. It was all in one stock, on one stock exchange in New York. I'd spent nine years building up Wizard and what I had to show was a swag of shares in a single company based thousands of kilometres away.

I had to start from the basics and learn fast. So in 2005 I decided to find out what I should do to give me a better spread of investments for risk, and to properly fund my retirement. I didn't know what I was doing: my expertise had been in building companies, in borrowing and lending money (which have nothing to do with stock markets) and in property development. I'd never been a holder of shares. I'd played the stock market, I'd got burned and I'd stayed away from the whole industry. I thought that investing in the stock market was about hearing a hot tip and punting on it. That's what I thought the stock markets were—sort of like the horses or betting on footy games.

I had no idea about where to find an adviser, a broker, a planner or a manager. Or, more accurately, I didn't know how to find a good one.

In early 2005 I approached a group of financial institutions based on their reputations and on what I perceived were their strengths. They were five investment banks/stockbrokers—Deutsche Bank, Merrill Lynch, Macquarie Bank, UBS Warburg and Goldman Sachs—and two managers of hedge funds, QED and Ellerston. I met with them and gave them all the same information about me.

The hedge funds were simple—I gave them the money and they invested it, and they told me the performance every quarter. But the investment banks and stockbrokers were different: they all assessed me for something called my 'risk profile' before advising me on an investment strategy. Surprisingly, all five of them were assessing the same person using risk profiling, yet came back with totally different strategies: Macquarie recommended I invest 100 per cent in Australian shares; Deutsche told me 20 per cent Aussie shares with the balance split among local and international professional investors (managed funds); Goldman Sachs advised 30 per cent Australian shares and the rest in various international markets. And so on.

I was intrigued. Why did they all have different strategies for me after doing my risk profile? Maybe this thing called a 'risk profile'—which I will elaborate on later—and the strategies that flow from it were not exactly the science we've been led to believe. Some of them had to be wrong.

I decided to split my money between all five and give them two years to see who I would continue with—who could make me comfortable and create good returns for retirement.

What I learned from these experts is really what this book is all about: that in order to retire with anything approaching enough money and assets to fund a comfortable and fulfilling retirement, you need three things: property, adequate superannuation, and your own independent investment portfolio of shares.

It doesn't matter if you're a 45-year-old worker who's never thought much about the future, or a small business owner working to build a nest egg, or a chief executive of a multibillion-dollar company approaching retirement—you need all three.

How to balance these and how to make sure you have the right amount of money tied up is a lifelong journey requiring passion, courage and wisdom. It's the Yellow Brick Road to your financial security.

There's also the 'ultimate investment'—the investment in yourself.

There are people out there retiring on $2 million, but their health is so bad they can't enjoy it. There are people who've concentrated so hard on the money that they've totally forgotten about their physical, mental and spiritual wellbeing. They're rich but they're not wealthy.

The ultimate investment is about acknowledging that, just as you incrementally finance a home before you retire and incrementally acquire shares and methodically build your super, so too can you piece together a strategy that will see you fit and healthy and able to enjoy your life by the time you retire.

These four investments will be covered in detail in this book. Once you have finished reading, I hope you walk away understanding your personal retirement strategy.

Every Australian needs to understand their personal retirement strategy

I obviously don't know about every reader's personal circumstances. I don't want to tell anyone that they can get rich quick—*they can't*. I don't pretend that everyone who reads this book can be as wealthy as someone who earns a lot more money than them. I'm not a motivational guru.

I don't have The Answer, and I urge you to be sceptical of those who claim to have it for you.

What I want to do in this book is take you through what I believe to be the issues and get you thinking. If nothing else, I hope the book gets you curious and asking questions of fund managers and financial advisers.

No-one but you can decide what the priorities are going to be for your own life. No single plan or outlook fits all circumstances and personalities. If you take two women, both 40 and earning the same money and living in the same city, you're going to find an entirely different outlook for the one who's on her second marriage and contemplating having more kids from the one who's single and has no kids and no house to worry about. The 50-year-old man starting a new family with a new wife—and with grown-up kids already living away from home—is thinking about things very differently to the man who's entirely focused on an early retirement. The goals of a 40-year-old are very different to the goals of a 60-year-old.

Everyone is different, but the issues are usually the same: How much do I need to retire on? What can I do? What are my goals? What is my strategy? What are the dangers?

I come from a conservative background, and I've had some success and some luck with investing and building companies and financing projects. Most of my success has come down to basic concepts and good preparation. I advocate a simple three-part approach to building any kind of wealth:

1 Goal
2 Strategy
3 Discipline.

It's not very sexy and it's not new. But it's the way I've approached everything, including my attempt to get my retirement savings sorted out. I don't care what you're trying to do or achieve in your own investments, it should follow the three-part approach. You should know where you're trying to get to, know how it's going to be achieved, and be confident that you have what it takes to follow through. As you save more money, more people are going to try to tell you what to do with it. Your job is to run these offers through your three-part test.

I hope to bring a unique view to building wealth and retirement planning by giving you an insider's knowledge of the investment industry and showing you some of the information that's usually reserved for the truly wealthy. I thank the high-powered advisers, bankers, financial planners and stockbrokers for the insights and secrets they shared with me, knowing that I'd write a book on what they disclosed. It may be of interest to readers to know that many of these advisers to the rich are as worried as I am at the lack of knowledge and understanding that most Australians have about retirement planning.

I'll also disclose my own experience and insights from 25 years as a property buyer and developer who has built everything from townhouses to hotels. There are basic tenets of property investment that every Australian should know. Again, I won't be showing any get-rich-quick schemes: property is a genuinely lasting and profound form of personal wealth, but it has to be approached with discipline and with no trace of short-term thinking.

I trust that by the end of this book you'll be armed with ideas.

1

THE BIG PICTURE

The research suggests that there is a huge gap between the expectations of baby boomers for their retirement and the financial reality of what they will be able to afford.

Simon Kelly, Principal Research Fellow at NATSEM

Most Australians don't think about a future when they won't be working. Well, at least, not in the way we should. We *do* think about what we might need in retirement, but inevitably the thinking is flawed.

The thinking is 'a house—I need a house for retirement'. And then many spend their working years buying and renovating the home and paying the mortgage. This is fine—property is the first step to a good retirement. But simply buying a house and paying it off is not really a strategy. In truth, it's not really investing either. For most people, buying a house is more like hoarding—you buy something, sit on it for 30 years and hope for the best.

Then there's speculation. We punt on shares as if this is a chance for real security when our working lives stop. People do this with property too. They chase quick capital growth, hoping they can buy low and sell high in a short timeframe. But this is not investment—it's really just speculation.

And more common than hoarding or speculation is what so many Australians do: nothing. The strategy is to just sit and hope that the government will pay the pension, or hope that the 9 per cent Superannuation Guarantee will be enough to retire on.

None of these are really plans for retirement; none of them come close to a strategy you can implement and rely on in old age. Hoarding, speculating and passively assuming that someone will look after you—these are based on hope. And anything with hope at its heart cannot be considered a strategy.

I didn't set out to write a book that scares people. However, any book that investigates solid strategies for retirement has to start with the facts. The first fact is that, with a bit of luck, we'll all grow old.

Growing old gracefully

Not only does each person hope to get old, as a nation we're getting older. The life expectancy for Australians has been increasing over the last hundred years so that people who are teenagers now can look forward to living into their eighties. The Report of the NSW Chief Health Officer (2006) said that, in the 35 years to 2004, life expectancy for men increased by twelve years and for women by ten years.

The ageing of the population will become particularly

noticeable by the mid twenty-first century, when there will be almost as many people over the age of 50 as there will be of 50 years or less. This contrasts with 2002, when less than one-third of the population was over 50. Australia's population has aged significantly in the last 130 years. In 1870, 42 per cent of the population was less than fifteen years old, compared to 21 per cent in 1998. The proportion of the population aged over 65 simultaneously increased from 2 per cent in 1870 to 12 per cent in 1998. By 2047 around 25 per cent of all Australians will be over 65 years of age.

In the United States, the Census Bureau expects 214,000 centenarians by 2020. One in nine US baby boomers may live to be 100, whereas at the end of World War II only one in 500 made it.

You don't need to be a genius to see that with an ageing population there are increasingly fewer working age people who are paying taxes to fund a full age pension. Not that the pension is enough to live on. But once we get to a point where the tax burden is too great for a broad-based age pension, the pension will cease to be something to rely upon for all except the most needy. If you doubt this, have a look at what's happening to the pension—it's been eroding, in real terms, for years.

You can't comfortably retire on the pension

The dilemma is this: to fund a broad-based age pension in an era when half of the population is over 50 will require either an increase in income tax or an increase in GST. Increasing income tax enough to make a difference, apart from being politically unpopular, creates incentives to avoid working and evade tax. Increasing the GST by the amounts required, which currently would be akin to political suicide, will hurt retirees with finite incomes—the same people you were trying to help. What is more likely to happen is an end to the age pension for all except the truly needy, and more tax *breaks* in super to get people contributing. In fact we're already seeing that happen. The federal government pushed through superannuation changes which took effect in 2007 that provided big tax incentives to put money into superannuation, particularly if you're over 50.

The point is that living on the age pension, which is currently around $200 a week (or a little over $11,000 a year for an individual and $23,000 for a couple), isn't something many people reading this would want to contemplate.

The era of defined benefits is gone

There's something else we can clear up: it's highly unlikely that anyone reading this is going to be retiring on a guaranteed amount of money. Many older Australians have grown up with what used to be called 'defined-benefit' pensions. These were lumps of money paid to employees on reaching a certain age, or a certain milestone of service. You could put in extra along the way, and an actuary would calculate how much your pension would be worth in 30 years if you put a certain amount extra in each week, indexed against inflation. Government departments, in particular, attracted people with the promise of a good pension plan, sometimes with early payouts. Police services and fire departments have always recruited this way. But in the last 25 years, all western economies have shifted from defined-benefit pensions—where the employer guaranteed a lump sum payout on a certain date—to 'defined-contribution' pensions (also called accumulation plans).

This trend has been particularly pronounced in Australia, where our superannuation system is now based on defined-contribution schemes. Defined contribution means, simply, that rather than an employer committing to how much they'll pay you on a certain date, now they're only committing themselves to how much they will contribute to your fund at certain intervals. In effect, the change works like this: rather than promise to pay you $800,000 when you turn 60 and retire, the employer—as required by the superannuation law—now contracts to pay you 9 per cent of your salary into the super fund of your choosing.

That's it—that's the obligation.

The era of defined-contribution schemes marks a big shift in responsibility. I'll go into this in more detail in Chapter 5, on super, but for now these are the two things we must never forget:

1 The retiree is now an investor.
2 The investor is responsible for all the risks.

As governments shifted from defined benefits to defined contributions, they also shifted the responsibility from the employer to the employee. Once, all of the responsibility lay with the employer: they promised to pay a certain amount on a certain day and the employee couldn't care less if the fund managers behind the scheme had a few bad years and were losing money for the employer. The employee still got paid.

There are only a handful of government or corporate defined-benefit schemes left in Australia, and those that are still operating are in 'run-out' mode. That is, there are no new members and the funds are merely paying out those who are still members. Defined-benefit schemes are the dinosaurs of our new, deregulated economy. And the new wave is defined-contribution schemes.

Now don't get me wrong. I think the Superannuation Guarantee (SG) scheme is good for the nation. There's no way Australia could have afforded to continue with the defined-benefit schemes. Under SG, it's mandatory that employees put 9 per cent of their wage into super. It's put away in a compounding fund for when the recipient is retiring. It's also tax effective: you get taxed less on money you put into a superannuation fund. When you take it out at the end, there's no tax on receiving the money. And while it's earning money in the fund, it's taxed at a concessional 15 per cent—much less than if it were taxed as income. In the end, it's about recognising what's good for you and acting on it.

However, super is not all good, and this is where we have to understand the Australian worker's new status as investor and risk-taker. Australia's 9 per cent 'Superannuation

Guarantee' is a confusing term. It doesn't guarantee any return or payment when you retire—it doesn't *define* a benefit. The only thing the Superannuation Guarantee guarantees is that the employer pays 9 per cent of your wages into a complying super fund.

This is how the risk has been shifted: *you* select the fund, *you* select the mix of investments, and *you* carry the risk that there won't be enough in there when you want to stop working. And that brings me to my third point.

You are responsible for your retirement

Yes. That's right. You are responsible for your retirement. And most people don't get any instructions about how to do it. When you learn to ride a bike you get training wheels. When you learn to drive a car you get L plates and P plates. But when you are told to look after your financial security, arguably the most important thing outside your family and health, you get no instructions. There you have it.

The average wage in this country is about $54,000, and, assuming that you work until you're 64, you'll need between $1.5 million and $2 million to fund a lifestyle that has become accustomed to that sort of income, depending on how you structure your retirement income and at what rate you run down your saved capital (retirees generally need 70 per cent of their peak earning years' salary).

So the mission set for you by the government is to save up to $2 million. Hands up anyone who knows how to do that?

The current 9 per cent will leave a 25-year-old, on average earnings, with about $750,000 when they retire. So there's a shortfall of at least $1 million and as much as $1.25 million.

Don't get scared by this. Just consider it one of the issues you have to address when you create your strategy. It's always good to remind yourself what you're working for.

The four investments

If you can take these basic facts on board then we can start to move to the heart of this book. And this is it: I believe that, in order to retire comfortably, Australians need four things:

- **Property:** The cornerstone of wealth, your guarantee of security, a place to live and an asset to borrow against or sell if dire circumstances demand it.
- **Superannuation:** An important accumulation with tax advantages, a legally mandated contribution scheme that in most cases involves the professional investment skills of financial advisers or fund managers. You have to do it anyway, so make the most of it.
- **Share portfolio:** A chance to build an independent wealth profile and one that not only creates additional income streams in retirement but also gives you a natural diversification against your superannuation and property. You also get an important flexibility with your

own portfolio—super is locked in and property has to be sold in one entire lot, whereas your share portfolio can be accessed whenever you want and you can do it in fractions.

- **Good health:** If you retire at 60, you have several decades of living ahead of you. Your health, wellbeing and happiness will dictate—every bit as much as your financial position—how fulfilling these years will be.

That's it. No bells, no whistles, no promises and no nonsense. This is the basic matrix of what you'll need in retirement. You want a place to live which is unencumbered by debt, you need investments that create income to replace your working-life salary, and you need good health to enjoy your retirement.

For every reader there will be a different mix of these financial assets. In the old days the motto was 30/30/30—that is, by retirement one-third of your wealth should be in property, one-third in shares and one-third in cash.

These days, with the amount of personal wealth tied up in property, this is unrealistic. If a person retires with $3 million in total wealth, it's quite likely that they will have 50 per cent of that wealth in property and most of the rest in shares, given that superannuation funds invest in shares and most personal portfolios are also invested in shares, not cash.

Times have changed. The important thing is that you understand what you're doing and why you're doing it.

2

WEALTH CREATION

No book on preparing for retirement would be complete without canvassing the following four points. I call them 'Key Concepts':

1 Income
2 Risk
3 Diversification
4 Market sentiment.

When you become responsible for something as important as funding your retirement, you take on the job of understanding not only everything you do, but everything you hire a professional to do for you. When I set out to write this book, I realised that what I didn't want to do was write a 'how to' book. I'd much rather produce something that talks about the issues, the fundamentals and the thinking behind investing rather than a guru-style approach. I think following people who claim to have all the answers is dangerous. I think it's much smarter to view things in a deeper, issues-driven way.

Face it—no-one in the investing community knows everything about everything, so don't look for that person. And also, don't expect that that person has to be you.

Whether you're trying to work out what fund you invest in or you're looking to buy an investment property, think in basics first. Think in terms of Key Concepts, rather than 'The Answer'. Because you know what? Sometimes 'no answer' is the answer. Sometimes there's no simple way through; sometimes the problem unfolds as a series of issues, and you'll have to treat the answer as a series of revelations. When the problems occur—and they always do—it's better to have understanding than a quick-fix. Just as 'goal, strategy and discipline' are the key to achieving financial security, 'income, risk, diversification and market sentiment' should decide why you invest. I see them as Key Concepts because they should underlie every decision.

Income

It seems like every time I read anything to do with personal finance in the Australian media someone is talking about diversifying portfolios and understanding your risk profile. These are important topics—they colour all of your decisions and, more importantly, they set some boundaries. But what concerns me is the lack of focus on what I consider to be our primary asset—the ability to create income. This comes at the top of the tree in my thinking, and I think it should for you too. The ability to create income is your most important asset, and you should be aware of the power this gives you. I've already warned that this book may be more about changing the way you see the world than any get-rich-quick schemes, and income is one example of this. It makes me annoyed when I hear someone complaining about their job as if it was getting in the way. Let's get it straight: income is what fuels all of your plans, funds your investments, repays your mortgage and allows you to live. All your strategies rely on income, so I think it's worth showing some respect for your ability to earn it.

This applies to everyone. If you have fifteen years of working life left or 45 years, you still have the ability to create income, not just for today but for your retirement.

A 50-year-old, or a 60-year-old, who hasn't thought much about retirement and hasn't saved much money still has the ability to contribute to their retirement years. Maybe it means giving up some luxuries now, or living in a smaller house to reduce the mortgage, or taking on a second job. But they still have the ability to earn income and put money aside for their retirement.

Take the case of Chris and Margaret, two 50-year-olds who've been married for 25 years. They each earn the average income of $54,000 a year, and combined have total super of $140,000. They figure they'll be able to live on an income of about $60,000 when they retire. The bad news is that if they retire at 65, then they'll have run out of money by the time they're 77. After that they'll have to rely solely on the age pension, which is about one-third of their $60,000 goal.

But if they both salary sacrificed just 5 per cent of their income to super (or paid an extra 5 per cent in super) for the final fifteen years of their working lives, their super and pension combined would allow them to live on $60,000 a year until they reach 81 years of age before they are solely dependent on the pension.

Young people have that thing that becomes very rare as you get older: they have time. They can work an extra job, they can travel interstate to chase money, and they can do endless overtime without having to worry about spouses and kids. They can also go to university or TAFE to secure better income in the future, and because they're young some of the mistakes they make won't have the same impact or gravity. Youngsters in particular should be encouraged to see their ability to generate income as a blessing and not something to be avoided. Let's say a 20-year-old starts working today and he has 45 years until retirement. Let's say he earns the average salary and that in his lifetime, taking into account inflation and rising wages, he'll earn $5 million. That's a big lump of money.

The other way to look at income is to look at what you'd need in assets to replace it. If a person is earning $80,000 a year right now, she'd need $1.6 million of investment residential real estate to replace the $80,000 (at a standard 5 per cent per annum rental yield). How many people have access to $1.6 million? Yet the same person who wouldn't know where to get $1.6 million cash to invest at 5 per cent is already making $80,000 a year. And she didn't have to buy the asset or save $1.6 million; she was given it. She was born with the ability to go out and work.

So income is valuable and should be treated as such. In my opinion, being focused on your income will naturally make you focused on finding a way to invest some of that income so that the investment eventually works as hard as you do. If you don't value the time and effort you devote to earning the money, you won't be so focused on making the money give back to you.

I have a simple way of talking to kids about their work or careers, or whatever they want to call their working lives. I say 'don't see it as a job—see it as cash flow'. If cash flow doesn't mean anything, try 'return' or 'yield'. Try using any other word than 'job' or 'work', which both tend to create negative connotations in so many minds. So let's call it your cash flow; your cash flow is your income stream for the rest of your life. Either it's funding your life right now, or it's funding the assets for your retirement, or it's the yield coming from the assets you've built up while you were working. Whichever part of the cycle you're in, it's cash flow. It's just that when you're still in your working years, you can be doing so much more about how much cash flow you're generating than in your retirement years. Generally speaking, you can't crank up property and share yields overnight: the markets for those assets will not respond to anything you can do. But you can make immediate and large changes with your work income. You can work harder, get educated, change jobs, work two jobs, work overtime; if you're self-employed you can take an extra risk, take on more staff, expand, etc. These are all things that people with retirement portfolios can't do. But you can do it if you're a 25-, 35-, 45- or 55-year-old person in the workforce. Even if you have only a few years left in the workforce, you can still make a significant difference to your retirement years.

So these are the years of elastic earnings of the type that you won't have in retirement. Once you respect this fact then the next step will be to demand that your cash flow is converted into something that works as hard as you do. And that's the real subject of this book: converting your current cash flow into something that works so hard that it creates cash flow in your retirement without you having to work for it—it will be working for you.

Risk

There are two main points here and they are risk profile and diversification. Anyone who's read any retirement planning literature would have seen these phrases. Let's start with risk profile: it's usually among the first things that financial advisers do when they take you on as a client. They ask you to fill out a questionnaire, from which they create a 'profile' of what kind of risks you're comfortable with. The profiles developed from these questionnaires are packaged into neat documents and presented to you as your risk profile. The risk profile forms a sort of guide on how the adviser will advise you. You will fall into one of five broad categories: at the two extremes are 'aggressive' (taking the biggest risks for the biggest return) and 'risk averse' (investing safely in cash, fixed-interest or 'defensive' investments). The other three categories sit on a spectrum in between.

Of course, people in their twenties and thirties are more likely to be in the 'aggressive' category, because time is on their side. Retirees or people approaching retirement, aware that their investment time horizon is shorter than someone in their thirties, are more likely to avoid volatility and take less risk with their investments. They're more likely to want 'defensive' investments.

What you need to understand is that risk has two sides to it. There is the amount of risk you're willing to take, and there's the amount of risk inherent in specific investments. The financial adviser's job is to match the two. If you don't want risk in your portfolio, you buy defensive assets but limit your ability to grow your investment.

When you take on extra investment risk, it means that you're prepared to accept fluctuations in the value of your investment in return for better results over the longer period. And if you take on highly risky investments in the hope of long-term rewards, you need to know that some high-risk investments may provide no return at all—they may fall over.

In between these extremes of aggressive and risk averse are the three shades of risk profiles. They go by various names depending on who you're investing with. Usually the more cautious profile of the moderate segment is called 'conservative' and the more adventurous of the moderates is called 'dynamic' or 'growth' or even 'dynamic growth'. In the middle of the road, answering the need for reasonable returns but with low volatility, is the 'balanced' or 'moderate' profile.

So, the five risk profiles look like this:

- Risk averse
- Conservative
- Balanced
- Growth
- Aggressive.

To help you recognise where you fit on the spectrum, here is a detailed description of the five profiles.

1 **Risk averse:** Your primary goal is to make sure you don't lose money, so you look for investments where the principal amount won't be eaten away. That means cash, such as bank accounts, and fixed-interest investments, which you buy and hold. You don't get capital gains on these investments but they're very safe.
2 **Conservative:** Your primary goal is for your investments to grow enough to offset the effects of inflation. This means investing in cash and fixed interest with a small proportion of growth assets, such as blue-chip shares. You'll receive interest income, and the value of the shares will (hopefully) rise. Often you'll also receive dividends from the shares, which provide extra cash and have some tax benefits (known as franking credits).

3 **Balanced:** You want a balance between the safety of interest income and the potential for share price appreciation and dividends (plus franking credits). You definitely want returns better than inflation. Around 40 per cent of your investments will be in cash and fixed interest and the rest in a mix of property (usually listed property companies on the stock exchange), Australian shares and international shares. Your investments will have a moderate amount of price volatility over a three- to five-year growth period.
4 **Growth:** You're willing to accept more volatility in the value of your investments in expectation of better results. About 20 per cent of your investment will be in cash and fixed interest and 80 per cent will be spread across property (usually listed property), Australian shares and international shares. Usually the largest portion will be in Australian shares. Your investing horizon is longer—normally more than five years.
5 **Aggressive:** You're willing to forgo price stability to create wealth. The large bulk of your investment is in growth assets, like property, Australian and international shares, and even riskier alternative investments such as private equity and derivative products. You should expect volatility in the value of your portfolio, and you need a long-term investment horizon of seven to ten years.

The five categories show the trade-off in risk and returns. And this is how simple the risk profile really is.

LIQUIDITY

One other thing you need to be aware of, and that's liquidity. Liquidity is the ability to buy and sell when you want at a price that properly reflects the value of the asset. Broadly, cash is highly liquid and private equity is highly illiquid. Managed funds are generally accessible within one to two weeks. Direct shares can be sold and funds received within four days.

Risk profiling

Risk profile questionnaires are standard forms, used by all financial services professionals. You can find questionnaires online by googling 'risk profile questionnaire', and many of our financial institutions give them away as background literature. You're telling the adviser the story of yourself—it's your own information and, more importantly, it's your own feelings about how you see investing and money and risk.

In keeping with my recommendations that readers intimately understand their own strategies, I suggest that everyone does their own risk profiling exercise so they know where they sit on the risk/return/volatility curve. Your adviser will often want to do their own. Under the Corporations Act, the adviser must match product outcomes to a client's needs, goals and objectives, and the adviser needs to understand an individual's risk profile to do that. But a warning: don't pay extra to an adviser just to get your risk profile done. That should be part of the service of seeing a financial adviser, and there's no way you should have to pay extra for it.

Another thing to remember about risk profiles, particularly ones conducted by third parties, is that most of the questions are qualitative—that is, they ask you to assign a level of feeling or emotion to certain scenarios or statements and for you to rate yourself. But a good adviser should be focused on what you *need* as well as what you *feel*. There should be a happy balance between the two. Not only do humans tend to underrate or overrate themselves on qualitative self-assessment tests, but once the answers have been given, another person interprets what the answers mean and advises on what's needed. Earlier I highlighted what happened to me in this respect: I gave all the same responses to the investment banks I approached, and they all came back with different strategies. It shows that risk profiling and the subsequent investment strategy is an art, not a science. If you conduct a risk profile on yourself, it can be a good guide to how comfortable you feel with risk.

Some financial planners simply attribute risk profiles based on lifecycle, or how many years you have until retirement. The big industry super funds often do this as a way of saving on financial adviser bills for their members. They invest in superannuation money based on the age of the contributor. There are generally five categories based on years until retirement. If you've got more than 25 years until retirement, your super fund is full of Australian and international equities, but if you are about to retire, your fund is 100 per cent cash investments. As members get older, their money is automatically shifted into more conservative assets.

It might sound sensible at first reading, but remember that a 65-year-old will still live for (hopefully) many years, and you still need your portfolio to grow. Unless you have plenty of money when you retire, and most people don't, then you still need your money to work for you and grow. That means not being totally defensive.

Try risk profiling yourself into one of the five profiles described above. In short: aggressive is for people who have the time and the ability to weather risk in exchange for the potential of capital growth returns—let's say more than ten years; risk averse is for conservative people, often already retired, who need regular, certain income. The investments that follow from this are largely self-selecting into two types of investments:

1 Investment for income (risk averse)
2 Investment for capital growth (aggressive).

Most investment portfolios will be a mix of both.

My own risk profile is pretty much in the middle of the pack: I want solid returns but I don't want to be in investments with high volatility. I don't see myself as an expert on the share market, so I don't want to be panicked by things I don't understand. For me, that sort of up-and-down experience would spoil any sense of financial

INFLATION RISK

One thing that many of the fund managers don't talk about is 'inflation risk'. Inflation discounts the value of money by about 3 per cent per year. So if you bought a commodity for $670 today, the same thing in ten years would require about $1000. Your savings sitting in a fixed-interest fund 'earning' 4 per cent are actually *returning* you closer to 1 per cent in real terms. And then tax is payable on your earnings. So sometimes risk averse is the riskiest thing of all. I understand perfectly why fund managers are not shouting this message from the rooftops: their members in the low-yielding cash management and fixed-interest accounts are already scared. To frighten them even more about inflation risk might be counter-productive. Still, readers should know this stuff and know that this can make the risk profile seem a little nonsensical. Perhaps keep it simple and see it this way: in investing, as in life, the real risk lives at the extremes of the spectrum. I deal with inflation risk in more detail later. (See Chapter 5.)

security I've worked hard for. Other people are different—they don't mind the volatility of a share-heavy portfolio, or they mind to such a degree that they want none of their investments in shares.

My basic risk-assessment process for all things goes like this: risk is not the likelihood that something bad will happen. Risk is the likelihood that something bad will happen *times* the gravity of the outcome of that event. For instance, someone may argue to me that the risk of a parachute failing during skydiving is infinitesimal. I look at the gravity of the parachute not opening rather than simply its likelihood. The gravity of a failed parachute opening is death. In the same way, when investing it's not so much 'what is the likelihood of losing money?' It's more like 'what is the gravity of losing my money, or a lot of it?' I'm conservative with money, so I tend towards a style of investment where there's a low likelihood of losing my money and a high likelihood that I'll make more than 10 per cent per year. So I stay close to equities—both foreign and local—but I focus on the income-producing and Top 50 stocks. That is, I like to see income (dividends) from shares and I only like the really big companies that are unlikely to take rollercoaster rides in price. At the same time, the likelihood of making very little return on my money is an absolute certainty if I put it all in cash. So I won't do that either.

What I've said in these last few sentences is in large part a risk profile. You can articulate the same view for yourself—the risk profile questionnaires can be the starting point, but you have to figure it out for yourself. In effect we all know what we're prepared to risk and what we're not, which is why I think you should take responsibility for the risk profiling part of your strategy. It puts you more in control, and prepares you better for my next topic.

Diversification

Diversification is intricately linked to a person's risk profile. If the risk profile tells you what volatility and performance you'll be comfortable with, diversification tells you where and how the investments have to be spread in order to achieve those rates of volatility and performance. Like many ideas in the investment world, diversification has become a cliché. But diversification is simply making sure there's a good mix of assets in your portfolio. A good mix of assets (and asset classes) allows your total portfolio to perform strongly over time even if individual components falter. For instance, historically when property booms, it's normal for the All Ordinaries Index (the measure of shares listed on the Australian Stock Exchange—ASX) to not perform so well. If you have both property and shares, you are diversified and your portfolio is protected from too much downside in one component. Same with fixed interest and cash: these return low but stable amounts year-in and year-out; they balance the high-risk element of the portfolio, such as property and shares. When interest rates go up, property markets cool down. But as those interest rates are going up, so are your returns from fixed-interest and cash investments, which are indexed off the same place that mortgage interest rates come from. So this is a diversification strategy too.

Then there is weighting—or the amount of money in one asset or asset class in a portfolio compared with another asset or asset class. Becoming 'overweight' in one area increases the risk in your overall portfolio. So inside general asset classes you then have to diversify to further protect your investments from being overweight in one area. In shares you might invest in middle-sized companies or international shares to offset your emphasis on Top 50 ASX stocks; in property you'll make sure you invest in commercial property trusts that have a geographical spread (some of them will even have an international flavour); in fixed interest, you might invest in a foreign fund as well as your Australian one and you might do the same for cash. Of course, some people have a high risk profile—they're chasing higher returns and are prepared to live with the volatility of having concentrations of types of asset classes.

There is another layer of diversification, and that's a manager's 'style'. When you invest in managed funds, the blurb on the PDS (product disclosure statement) includes some information on how the fund manager invests the pool of money. This breaks down into three basic types of fund management: growth (where the manager tries to outperform the market), value (where the manager looks for underpriced stocks that they believe will be revalued by the market) and index (where the manager matches a portfolio against major indices such as the S&P/ASX 200). You can see how a spread of these styles in your portfolio could also diversify your investments.

If a lot of your wealth is tied up in property, the best diversification strategy might be to use existing equity in your own home and/or your investment property to either borrow more and diversify your property holdings, or borrow and buy a share portfolio. Also, don't have all your property in one area or one type of property. You could buy several waterfront apartments when rents and capital growth are high for such places. But if the market turns—and it always does—you have no diversified holdings to prop up the portfolio while waterfront apartments do badly. Diversification helps you get through the tough times. It's an inbuilt insurance mechanism, creating a pocket of decent performance when other assets may be struggling.

I can't tell you what to do, because I'm not an adviser. But I can say that diversifying your investments—which essentially is taking out some insurance for your money—is really just common sense. Regardless of which asset class you're in, look at it in terms of what sort of mix you have: are you diversified by investment type? by geography? by your time horizon and liquidity? by returns and volatility? The cliché goes like this: don't put all your eggs in one basket.

Having understood this, remember that financial institutions have products that cater for diversified investing. Your basic 'balanced' superannuation fund, for instance, is a good example of this. The typical balanced fund contains:

Balanced	
Australian shares	35%
International shares	15%
Property	10%
Fixed interest	35%
Cash	5%

Individual fund managers could have these weightings slightly different, but you get the idea. Balanced funds are the ones expected to return between 7 per cent and 9 per cent per annum over the long term. And that doesn't include fees.

If you're confused about what a good asset allocation would be in your own portfolio, just see what the professionals do. The information is all there. Every fund manager has a PDS which has to lay all this out. You can order these documents and see how they do it. Their funds also buy specific things like Asian commercial property, European small companies, US bonds, Japanese equities . . . the list goes on. There's a fund for every investor, and all of them—in their own way—are diversified for the risk profile and the appetite of the investor. For the record, here are the extremes of Australian managed fund diversification, based on risk profiles:

Risk averse (defensive)	
Australian shares	0%
International shares	0%
Fixed interest	65%
Cash	30%
Property	5%

Aggressive	
Australian shares	35%
International shares	35%
Fixed interest	0%
Cash	5%
Property	25%

These are the typical funds, but you can see how risk profiles and diversification come together in the funds that are offered.

Market sentiment

Once you have your income sorted out and are aware of risk profiles and diversification, you're in a position to at least know that you have a certain amount to invest and that there are different places you can put your money which will produce different volatility and returns. Income, risk and diversification are Key Concepts. But so is the idea of 'market sentiment'. This refers to the mood of the market—whether it's trending up or down.

This may not apply so strongly when you invest via a super fund or managed fund, because market sentiment is something that you pay the professionals to follow. But if you have properties or your own share portfolio, you're going to have to at least keep a watching brief on what the market is doing. I'm not advocating that amateurs read a few economic reports and then pretend they're professional investors. In fact, as a general rule for executing an investment strategy I personally like the buy-and-hold approach. With both property and equities I believe in the saying about 'time in the market' being better than 'timing the market'. There are very few people who can consistently speculate in property or equities simply by buying and selling and make regularly good income. Generally you need to spend at least one year invested in any given share in order to start making money, and the longer you hold the share, the more likely you'll make money. You need to have a ten-year time horizon if you're hoping to make money by investing in a residential property. But you still need to understand market sentiment: you need this because it will decide the most important aspects of your investing in these classes, and that's when you enter and when you exit.

There are different ways of looking at market sentiment. You can look at it regionally, assessing things like political climate (is a council pro- or anti-development?) and historical growth. You can go by sector and look at what the view is on, say, banking in India; market sentiment for Indian banks is very strong right now because there's a deregulation-led rush for home mortgages. Or you can do general reading and research, which should include a daily trawl of sites on the internet, to get an idea of where a certain market or sector is in its cycle. Is it at the end or the beginning? Is it time to get on or time to get off? If a share market is at a six-year high, is this the time to be buying in? If another market is at a five-year low, is that the time to be selling?

Market sentiment is hardly a science—you have to listen to people on TV, read columnists, go on the internet and listen to radio news. You have to build a picture. It's not a science but I think it's very important in a capitalist economy. Market sentiment drives oil prices, housing, business borrowing and employment. These are quite aside from the quarterly inflation, retail, employment and housing starts data, and different again to interest rate announcements from the Reserve Bank. When looking at the property market I always keep a close eye on the key drivers of supply and demand: how many people have started building houses in the last quarter and what's the state government's forecast for housing demand? All of this is on the internet, and you can also get it by ringing the government departments. The trick is that every industry sector has its professional association and their websites always have the latest data. Strong inflation suggests the Reserve Bank will raise interest rates, as do stronger than usual economic growth figures. Fewer houses being built will mean an increase in rental yields in about a year's time. Low unemployment can signal the beginning of a rate-rise cycle because low unemployment usually means that economic activity could be in danger of overheating.

These are just observations. Your job is to follow a few of them, start piecing together bits of the puzzle, and then cross-check your own conclusions with those of advisers and commentators. Don't be egotistical about this—it's not a contest. You should build a consensus of sentiment without getting too confused. If there are two stock-brokers' newsletters, and they're often at odds with their picks and their market views, you should pick one and stick with it. If, on the other hand, you can't see any consensus, then don't do anything. I wouldn't invest when all the advisers and commentators are at odds over what an incident or announcement means for a stock or a sector.

I'd sit on my money and wait for there to be a pattern. That's why you read the media and advisers and analysts every day—to see how others view information and to test it against your own conclusions. This is the basis of understanding market sentiment—it's not science but I believe it's crucial for anyone who wants to play an active part in their investment strategy.

DAILY NEWS

I use the daily newspapers to appreciate market sentiment. I read the *Sydney Morning Herald*, the *Daily Telegraph* and the *Australian Financial Review*—mostly because they give me different perspectives on the same issues. I'm looking for obvious things like interest rate movements, inflation figures and economic growth numbers. But I'm also looking for stories about housing approvals, bankruptcy rates, migration and population numbers. All of these help me form an idea not of the dry economic data that most financial services professionals use, but an actual picture of what people are doing, how Australians are living their lives and what this might mean for my various investments. Some of the best investments I've made in property—and the property developments that followed—came from reading a newspaper and getting an idea.

Be an informed investor

As a way of ending this chapter, I'd like to alert you to the amount of do-it-yourself information there is online. There's never been a better time to be an informed investor in this country, and I urge you to see what's out there and start building your own understanding.

In particular I'm very impressed by the federal government's 'Understanding Money' website at www.understandingmoney.gov.au. For anyone who feels overwhelmed by how much there is to learn about investing for retirement, I think this site is a great starting point. It articulates the issues and does so in a way that helps rather than hinders. The other site that every investor should look at is another federal government site called MESI (Monthly Economic and Social Indicators) at www.aph.gov.au/library/pubs/MESI/mesi.pdf. This is a service from the Australian Parliament House Library which condenses all data into a single document, and it's updated once a month. It's exactly what you need when judging market sentiment because it covers everything from interest rate trends and inflation to housing starts and employment rates. And it's free.

3

GETTING STARTED

Those of us lucky enough to live full lives and grow old have retirement to look forward to one day. We know that the government considers the funding of retirement to be our responsibility—the current super system only guarantees the contribution made, not the benefit received. We also accept that for most of us the 9 per cent super contributions will not be enough to live on, that most retirement funding estimates assume an unencumbered home (which you might have to sell for a cheaper one), that you'll need other investments apart from super to create income in your retirement, and that your health and wellbeing—in the end—will be your biggest and most important asset.

The questions are: How are you going to put all this together? What are the steps to get you from where you are at the moment to where you want to be in retirement? Who can help you? What are the costs? How long will it take?

The most important thing you can take away from this book, in my opinion, is not a secret recipe for success but a new way of looking at your life. Whether you have $5000 or $50,000 or $500,000 saved, it's up to you to learn to be smart about your money. The average Australian income is about $54,000 and each individual, on average, has about $68,000 in super. This book is not about the easy way, the magic wand or the quick-fix. However, the tools and the tax laws and the information and the expertise all exist so that most people who are serious about it can put a strategy in place that yields them 70 per cent of their working-life income once retired.

I believe that the four-part investment scheme I showed you in the previous chapter is a template that will work for the majority of Australians. To recap, it involves:

1 Property
2 Superannuation
3 Share portfolio
4 Investment in yourself.

It's balanced, it's simple, it's diversified and it's realistic. But, like most things worth doing, it involves some sacrifice, some discipline, a commitment to work, and an ongoing interest in and responsibility for your plan. It also involves time since—as you'll learn in later chapters—I don't believe in overnight wealth.

So before we get to the technical aspects of putting the four-part investment strategy together, I think it's important that readers have their minds in the right place. There's a lot to be said for having your attitude right before you get on the field—ask any professional athlete.

Understand the strategy

As I said in the introduction, anybody with serious ambitions to create a solid platform for retirement has to not only have a strategy but also needs to understand it. As I went through my own education in these matters I was amazed at how many terms and figures and strategies I was introduced to that could easily have left me confused. I'm curious and I'm fussy about where my money is. I started life as a chartered accountant and I work in finance and the capital markets, so I ask questions. Lots of questions.

But I wondered how many other people—especially those without a financial background—were experiencing this and not asking the questions. I reckon a lot, going on some of the conversations I've had with many different Australians—and these are people who have a financial planner. Why don't they understand their own strategy? So here's the point: whether you adopt everything you read in this book, discard all of it, or use a bit here and there to streamline your own approach, you must understand your strategy and where it's taking you. The worst position you can be in—discounting the 'do-nothings'—is to become a speculator or a hoarder. Speculators and hoarders do not have a strategy—they think they do, but if you listen really carefully you realise they're both running on hope. And hope is not a basis for investment.

You need a strategy and you need to totally understand it. Even if your plan is to outsource all decisions to a fund manager, you should understand why you're selecting a particular fund, or why you consider yourself to be 'conservative' in terms of how much risk you want to take. If the strategy is to move away from your property interests and towards shares, why are you doing it? When you got your 'super choice' form from your employer, why did you write down 'AXA'? Why did you tick the 'balanced' box? I'm not saying you shouldn't have, but did you understand why you did it? The same thing goes for starting a self-managed superannuation fund (SMSF). It sounds like a great idea because it's sold on having flexibility and freedom and 'control over your investments'. But how does it fit with your broader strategy and goals?

One of the best ways of refining your strategy in your own mind is to try writing it down in one sentence. When you get to the point of being able to do this, you probably completely understand what you're trying to do. I put this concept of understanding at the top of the list because I think it's crucial: in your journey through the financial services maze you'll find a lot of people who'll urge you to do all sorts of things for what look like good reasons. Your job is to use these people to get where you want to go, rather than allow them to use you to take them where *they* want to go. And to do that you'll need to know exactly what it is that you want. Which brings me to the next point.

Set goals

Don't be put off by the idea of 'goal-setting'. There are guru-type advisers who talk about goal-setting, and these people can distract us from what is a sound technique for getting where you want to be. Goals don't have to be New Age or related to get-rich-quick schemes. You don't have to chant them or make the whole thing into a cult. Goals are what you put in place to ensure that the strategy you've developed has a focus. A strategy needs a goal. Write down your goals. The more you write down the goals the more you're testing the strategy, second-guessing your own numbers and constantly tweaking what you're doing. Committing goals to the page makes you focus and makes you get into a habit of checking performance indicators such as capital gains and yields. You can draw diagrams, you can create spreadsheets, you can use wealth-management software found online. There are so many tools these days for investors who want to get involved. Whatever you do, the important thing is to use a system that works for you so that the goals are not only in your mind, but are also aligned with your strategy. The way to think about this is to admit that your entire retirement savings plan is one large goal: you're aiming to have a certain amount of assets in your retirement to fund a lifestyle that costs a certain amount of money each year. You need a certain amount of assets to produce a certain amount of income each year. This is the ultimate goal—so be clear about it.

How much will I need?

How much will I need? It's one of the biggest financial questions we ask ourselves, and the hardest one to answer. But you can do some research yourself to start figuring it out. Go to the Australian Securities and Investments Commission (ASIC) website (www.asic.gov.au) and use their online retirement savings calculator. Start with something simple. Start with what you've got and what it will be worth in five, ten, 20 or 30 years' time. From there, you can work out how much you'll have to put away if you want to live a certain lifestyle, and then you can develop a goal and strategy.

There are other online calculators that take the opposite approach, telling you how much it will cost to retire, and then you have to work out how to save that much money. Check out the Westpac ASFA Retirement Living Standard calculator at www.westpacinfo.com.au/RLSCalculator. It's more basic than many of the calculators because it whittles the questions down to where you live, whether you want to live 'modestly' or 'comfortably', and whether you're male or female. It itemises the living expenses and also does everything in today's dollars—it assumes you will retire tomorrow.

If you input 'male' in 'Sydney, NSW', who wants to live 'comfortably', the calculator comes back with $675 per week, or $35,122.61 per annum.

As of late 2007, it looks like this:

Weekly breakdown of expenditure		
Housing (e.g. contents, insurance, rates, repairs)	$83.55	(12.37%)
Energy (e.g. electricity, gas)	$12.64	(1.87%)
Food	$128.64	(19.05%)
Personal care (e.g. hairdressing, makeup, personal care)	$14.20	(2.10%)
Household goods and services (e.g. furniture, household items, cleaning, tools)	$87.33	(12.93%)
Clothing and footwear (e.g. clothing, underwear, footwear)	$25.23	(3.74%)
Transport (e.g. car running costs, public transport)	$106.84	(15.82%)
Health services (e.g. health insurance, medical, dental, medicines)	$50.98	(7.55%)
Leisure (e.g. books, TV, computer, vacations)	$144.12	(21.34%)
Gifts and/or alcohol or tobacco	$21.89	(3.24%)
Total per week:	**$675.43**	
Total per year:	**$35,122.61**	

The calculator is very flexible, allowing plenty of options. For example, a single woman, retiring in Perth, will need approximately $369 a week to maintain a 'modest' lifestyle in retirement. The breakdown is as shown on page 51.

From these calculations we can already see how the decisions you make with your investments and planning at a younger age are going to affect you in retirement. The

Weekly breakdown of expenditure

Housing (e.g. contents, insurance, rates, repairs)	$72.45	(19.65%)
Energy (e.g. electricity, gas)	$13.30	(3.61%)
Food	$64.16	(17.40%)
Personal care (e.g. hairdressing, makeup, personal care)	$25.56	(6.93%)
Household goods and services (e.g. furniture, household items, cleaning, tools)	$50.12	(13.59%)
Clothing and footwear (e.g. clothing, underwear, footwear)	$14.06	(3.81%)
Transport (e.g. car running costs, public transport)	$71.89	(19.50%)
Health services (e.g. health insurance, medical, dental, medicines)	$12.10	(3.28%)
Leisure (e.g. books, TV, computer, vacations)	$45.05	(12.22%)
Gifts and/or alcohol or tobacco	$0.00	(0.00%)
Total per week:	**$368.68**	
Total per year:	**$19,171.59**	

difference between Sydney and Perth, male and female, and comfortable and modest is $100 or more a week in leisure expenditure. The difference between 'modest' and 'comfortable' is that you have no 'Gifts and/or alcohol or tobacco' in the budget. And the person living modestly in Perth has half the food budget of the person living comfortably in Sydney. Half!

So, let's change that to a couple, living in any area of Victoria, who wants to live comfortably. They'll need $922 per week, or $47,941.30 per annum.

Weekly breakdown of expenditure

Housing (e.g. contents, insurance, rates, repairs)	$83.41	(9.05%)
Energy (e.g. electricity, gas)	$14.45	(1.57%)
Food	$179.40	(19.46%)
Personal care (e.g. hairdressing, makeup, personal care)	$39.57	(4.29%)
Household goods and services (e.g. furniture, household items, cleaning, tools)	$94.21	(10.22%)
Clothing and footwear (e.g. clothing, underwear, footwear)	$56.43	(6.12%)
Transport (e.g. car running costs, public transport)	$109.53	(11.88%)
Health services (e.g. health insurance, medical, dental, medicines)	$98.63	(10.70%)
Leisure (e.g. books, TV, computer, vacations)	$202.92	(22.01%)
Gifts and/or alcohol or tobacco	$43.39	(4.71%)
Total per week:	**$921.95**	
Total per year:	**$47,941.30**	

As you can see from these examples, taken from the Westpac ASFA calculator, the cost of living if you retired tomorrow differs between regions and gender, and between expectations. I'm going to look at the cost of living in Sydney, because the cost of living in Sydney drives much of what happens in the national economy. (You might be interested to know that the calculator says a female retiring comfortably in Sydney needs $35,932.66—slightly more than the male figure because of the greater spending on personal grooming!)

Let's split the difference and say that to retire comfortably in Sydney tomorrow as a single person you'd need to find $35,000 a year. If you're a comfortable couple, you're looking for $48,000 per annum (on an Australia-wide basis, it's $30,000 per single person and $45,000 per couple).

What it really means

There are some points to remember when trying to plot the cost of retiring. The first that I notice from the Westpac ASFA calculator is the time-honoured assumption that to retire comfortably, with as few outgoings as possible, you'll need an unencumbered home. The Westpac ASFA calculator I have been using assumes this. This is why I started with property as the first focus of this book—you're going to want it when you retire, not only because of the security you get but to reduce rental and mortgage overheads.

The next thing you notice is that the Sydney 'comfortable' cost of retirement is around $35,000 per year, which is pretty close to my assumption at the start of this book that you'll need income of about 65 to 70 per cent of your peak adult earning years. Given that the average normal-time salary for Australian adults is now $54,000 per year, you can get the idea.

The other point is in the form of a question: What are these numbers going to be in 20 years' time? Or 30 years?

The cost of money is 'discounted' by 3 per cent per year, which is Australia's long-term inflation rate. We've had a few low inflation years, but it will come back up and it will average out. To get an idea of the kind of money you'll need in 20 or 30 years' time, use a compound calculator like the ones at the Commonwealth Treasury's Understanding Money site (www.understandingmoney.gov.au) or the ASIC site (www.fido.asic.gov.au). There you'll find that $35,000 now buys the same as $63,000 will buy in 20 years and $85,000 in 30 years. That's what you're going to have to find each year in retirement.

How will I get there?

The Westpac ASFA calculator views retirement planning from the practical perspective of how much income a person really needs to live in one of two ways, in a choice of locations. Then, giving this information a new value because of inflation tells you where you have to be in the future. And from there you have a chance to add back and find what you have to put away in order to have a sufficient income-generator in the form of a superannuation account.

As mentioned above, the best calculators I've seen for developing goals and testing what you'll need in retirement are probably at ASIC's Fido site, and the Understanding Money site. Have a good play around with some of these tools. You may have been underestimating what you could save for retirement; you may not have realised that just a few extra dollars here and there over the years would compound to much bigger amounts later.

Secondary goals

Beneath the big-picture goal of putting away enough money to have a comfortable retirement, you'll need secondary goals. These are shorter-term goals for each investment. For instance, you may have committed to buy an investment property before you're 30, 40, 50 or 65 years old; you may want to buy a boat, fund private school fees for your children or take a long holiday. The goal may be to jog a total of 20 km per week, or go for a year without having a cigarette. Having a hierarchy of goals—with the retirement day total at the top—is an important step. Once you've got your goals written down somewhere, you can tweak them.

Be disciplined

As we get further into this book, I'm going to suggest some techniques and strategies that you may not have considered or which you thought were only for very wealthy people. But before we get there, I must emphasise the need to have the right attitude. Once you know your goals and build a strategy around them, you have to stick with it. You can call this 'keeping your own promise' or 'having faith'; I use the word 'discipline'. It doesn't matter what word you use; what does matter is that once you've set your goals and chosen the strategy, you have to have the discipline to see it through.

This is perhaps the key difference between professional investors and the so-called 'mums and dads'. Professional investors are not usually traders or speculators. They're not hoarders either. Most professional investors have their goals and a strategy. But what really sets them apart is adhering to their model. If they're rebalancing every six months on certain criteria, then that's what they do. If—on a rare occasion—they decide to speculate on a stock and the stock starts to take off, they might sell as the stock rises. It takes enormous discipline to do this when a stock has gained, say, 20 per cent in a week. But that's the difference discipline makes. If one of their stocks falls in price they don't panic-sell. Why? Because the strategy says you don't sell stocks on a low.

Even though you're not a professional, you can adopt this discipline too. If for instance you don't have time for your own investments, and your strategy is to put an extra 5 per cent into super each month, then do it. You have the goal, you have the strategy, but it will be the lack of discipline that lets you down every time. The same goes for your investment in yourself: Australia's gyms are littered with exercise program cards that members had customised just for them by a fitness professional. There are three or four entries on the cards, and then they stop. The strategy and goals were in place, and they'd paid the gym fees, but there was no discipline.

If the best way to state your goals is to write them down, and the trick to understanding your strategy is to formulate it, then the best way to create discipline is to make it a habit. You can think about it like this: eating crappy food is a habit; ignoring your super and just letting your employer deal with it is a habit; leaving your mortgage on the same old settings is a habit. If these things are habits, they were formed by doing them over and over. So a new habit can be just as easily formed—a habit where your mortgage is paid weekly or your super is in a fund of your choosing or you're going to the gym three times a week. Make discipline a habit and pretty soon it won't feel onerous.

Consult an expert

Don't try to carry your entire strategy on your own back all the time. You need help from experts; you need people who can help you execute the plan in the way that you envisage. If you're investing in property, you need a lender and a solicitor and an accountant and perhaps a real estate agent to help you execute your plan. If you want to boost your super or build a share portfolio, you'll want a financial adviser to ensure that you're getting the most out of your investments. If you're on a health plan, who are you working with? We all like to be masters of our own destinies, but making a success out of a strategy depends—in the end—on how it's actually executed. It's a bit like a football team: the coaching staff can come up with the best strategy and prepare the players to the best condition of their lives. But if the players don't execute—if the players aren't good enough—then the strategy doesn't count for much.

My advice is to find the best people and have them do the execution of the significant parts of your strategy. Find the best real estate agents, solicitors, accountants, financial advisers, stockbrokers, bankers, property maintenance companies, trainers, dieticians and physicians. All of these professions probably know more about their specialty field than you do, and the time will come when you should use them to help you make the best decisions. Yes, they charge for their time and expertise, but baulking at paying experts who can help you achieve your goals is shortsighted.

I have one caveat on this general point: while I see the financial planning industry as very important, I have come to the conclusion that planners whose fees are paid by the fund managers of products they're recommending should be avoided. The Australian Consumers' Association (Choice) has done its own surveys on these planners and they have used the term 'structurally corrupt' to describe a system where a person purporting to give you unbiased advice on where to put your money is being paid a commission by the fund manager who subsequently gets your money. In this case—and this is how much of the financial planning industry works—the 'adviser' is not working for you; they're working for the fund manager who is paying them. Only it's not really the fund manager paying; it's you. The commission that goes to the financial planner comes out of your pocket, reflected in the higher fees you pay.

In some of the large financial planning dealer networks, the planners are penalised for putting clients into funds that don't pay the highest commissions to head office. So the planners, who like their bonuses as much as anyone, push their clients into funds that are paying the best commissions. If you doubt what I'm saying, just have a look at ASIC's seven-month investigation into Australia's largest financial planning network, AMP Financial Planning. The investments watchdog was looking into how well AMP handled the introduction of Super Choice in 2006 and found that when advising clients, the planner channelled the money into an AMP product 93 per cent of the time. In half of these cases, the planner failed to disclose a reasonable basis for the recommended switch. It's worth remembering that the planners were rewarded for putting more people onto head office's products, whereas industry funds pay no commissions to financial planners. You have to ask yourself—what has a remuneration policy like this got to do with *my* retirement strategy? Financial planning is a valuable and important business. A lot of financial planners are very good at what they do and are conscientious. But if they're working in a system that rewards them in the way it does, they'll be persuaded to do it that way.

I suggest that you use independent advisers who don't take commissions from fund managers, and if they do, they should rebate them back to you. Make sure your financial adviser can explain their fee structure and you can understand it and are comfortable with it. And make sure they don't get paid 'trailing commissions', where the fund manager pays the adviser a percentage of your money every year for not doing very much. Insist that your financial planner rebates any commission they receive from fund managers. If they don't, find a new planner. I'm not saying you'll get a cheaper service doing it this way. However, you have to find the best person to execute the strategy, and common sense tells us that that person should be working solely for your interests, rather than being an agent pushing the products of a fund manager who pays the highest commission.

You should also be aware of track record: What has my financial planner done? How long have they been operating? What type of clients do they deal with? What do people say about them? This goes for stockbrokers, doctors and real estate agents too. It's worth investigating that they're experts with track records in the areas you want to be in. If you want to trade only in Top 30 or Top 50 stocks on the ASX then it's pointless engaging a broker who's constantly trying to get you into 'penny dreadful' mining stocks or speculative stocks. If you want to invest in residential property in a certain area, walk around that area for a couple of weekends and see which real estate agents are representing which type of property. If you're committed to doing something about your health, do you really want a doctor who simply writes lots of prescriptions and tries to move you on as fast as possible, or do you want a physician who's prepared to work with you on your overall wellbeing?

4

PROPERTY

I have a general policy on property: buy and don't sell.

You can do a lot more with property if you have it than if you sell it. Look at the people who usually do well with property-based wealth and you'll see that they never sell. They buy well and they hold, they rent it out, they re-finance, they leverage properties for more purchases. But they don't sell.

As I said in Chapter 1, I believe all Australians must have an unencumbered home to create a successful retirement. That's the first building block. If they want to be doing better than most in retirement, they should have a rental property too.

There are many reasons why you need unencumbered property. And given that property is such a studied, analysed and written-about asset, the technical arguments about long-term capital growth and rental yield are fairly well publicised. I'll get into all that later.

But for a start, property is inherently a good asset in Australia, so long as you look at it as at least a ten-year investment. As an overview, you should remember these two points: residential property historically has outpaced both inflation and economic growth. If you want to go deeper, have a look at the figures produced by the Real Estate Institute of Australia (REIA). They show that between 1986 and 2006 the median house price in Australia increased 391 per cent, or an annual increase of 8.3 per cent while inflation rose at 3.6 per cent and the economy grew at an average pace of 3.4 per cent.

Let me give you the basics: you've probably heard people talking about the link between property and a happy retirement? Well, the owner-occupier component of this is self-explanatory: if you own the home you're living in, the after-tax income you're producing from other quarters is free cash flow, in that you're paying no rent or mortgage. This is one of the reasons that retirement income is formulated around 70 per cent of your peak adult earnings, and in some models as low as 60 per cent. You're not paying a mortgage or rent. Think about the house you're currently living in and how much it would cost to rent. For most people it's about one-third of their household income; a mortgage is about 40 per cent, but is eventually paid off. So a person who owns their own home when they retire is already between 30 and 40 per cent better off than their peers who don't own their own home. If on retirement you have an unencumbered house worth $1 million, its market rental would be about $1000 a week (5% of value per year). So the very simple fact of having a house with no mortgage and having no rent to pay is immediately making your retirement income go further. It also gives you a feeling of security.

Second, a debt-free property you live in is inflation-proof and interest-rate-proof (over ten-year periods). You've seen those graphs about how much money you'll need in order to live in 20 years' time, and you get confused about the difference between 2008 dollars and 2028 dollars? Having a house with the loan paid off gets around any of that confusion because the 2028 value of rent won't matter and neither will the 2028 interest rate. You own the place; all the equity is yours. You can sell it and buy a smaller house, putting the money left over into your retirement fund. You can move out into a smaller place and rent your home out. You can take in a lodger.

Third, the freehold house is an emergency fund. I don't advocate going into debt as a retiree, but if worse ever comes to worst, your unencumbered property is something that can be mortgaged to create funds.

So the debt-free home creates the security and increases available cash flow. It's also a safety net. And if you add to this scenario an investment property and hopefully a share portfolio, you're creating the other thing we all want in retirement—an income stream.

Let's say on retirement—in fifteen years' time—your two-bedroom rental apartment that you looked so hard for, and which was so stressful to afford when you first bought it, is now valued at $1 million. At a rental value of 5 per cent of value, you would be making about $1000 a week before tax. This is quite aside from your superannuation fund, which was built up through the guaranteed contributions your employer made and anything extra you put in. Add in the share portfolio that you've built up over a number of years and you should be able to fund a comfortable retirement.

Another popular scenario for people who've retired is to move into a smaller house that they finance with their unencumbered main home, and then rent out the main home. Once again, you get income and you have a place to live in that has already been paid for.

Clearly, having a serious strategy for property, and sticking with it, is a good idea. And it should be at the centre of all your strategies for these reasons: it's an asset class that isn't as volatile as the share market and you have some control over it; it's an asset that can be sold if you really need to, although it's not as liquid as shares; you can borrow against it to create more wealth; you can live in it; and a debt-free home is largely inflation-proof (except for the cost of rates and maintenance) and it's protected from interest rate fluctuations.

So in retirement you need a debt-free place to live in, and you'd really like to have a debt-free investment property as well.

Starting out

I have assumed that anyone interested in a good retirement is going to buy a property to live in at least, and maybe an additional investment property. But perhaps some people have left it late, or not thought about it, or have not been in a position to do so previously.

My observations about getting started in the property market are that too many people stand on the sidelines dithering, and too many also leap in expecting to make a lot of money quickly. Avoid acting like either of these. Property is at least a ten-year proposition—any less than this is not going to get the results you want. Conversely, standing on the sidelines, forever second-guessing the market and worrying about where interest rates and prices are going, is also going to get you nowhere.

In my opinion, money is not a thinking word, it's an action word. You have to act—you have to make the leap at some point. I believe that we're in a historically stable period as far as interest rates go. The years in which I witnessed interest rates going from 6 per cent to 17 per cent I believe are gone. The western world is now in a low-interest rate environment and I can't see anything that's going to change that in the near future. The last five years have seen 6 per cent as the benchmark rate, and interest rates will revolve around this number for a while to come. The wild ride of rates going from 6 per cent to 17 per cent and down again was a structural adjustment. Rates shouldn't jump like that any time soon, thanks to historically low and stable inflation. I wouldn't be holding my breath for rates to go to 3 per cent, but nor do I think they'll go into double figures. So, in this environment, the main things that are going to change are how much you can save, how much you can earn, and how much extra you can put on your mortgage.

Regardless of this longer view, the whole emphasis should be on making sure that you've done your homework, that you have goals and a strategy, and that you're committed to the discipline required to see your plan through.

For first home buyers, let me take you through the basics:

1 You need to find out how much you can afford to repay to a mortgage lender.
2 You need to start establishing a savings history.
3 You have to declare all your debt—including store cards, credit cards and car finance—and get rid of as much of it as possible.
4 Use websites such as www.wizard.com.au or www.asic.gov.au to see how much you can borrow.
5 Then you need to find the deposit amount and decide what your starting equity in the property will be. Aim for at least 20 per cent to avoid mortgage insurance and higher interest rates.
6 Don't forget to save for the legal fees and other costs, like stamp duty, that come with buying a house.

My advice to anyone who's been standing on the sidelines is to get the requisite savings together, find the place you can afford, and then buy it. It may not be the dream house, and it may not be in the suburb you wanted. It may be $100,000 cheaper than the home you wanted to be in. But you have to start at the beginning in property and you

FLEX YOUR MUSCLES

You should get a mortgage facility with the flexibility to alter things as your life changes—change payment frequency, change payment amount, deposit lump sums without being penalised, pay out early without being penalised, and free and unlimited redraw. The most flexible is usually the standard variable rate mortgage. It's slightly more expensive than the basic variable rate, but I believe the flexibility is worth paying extra for.

I am opposed, by the way, to fixed rate mortgages. I can see the use for them in business lending and investment properties, because you know exactly how much interest you will pay. But with your house, fixed rates are almost always going to be more expensive than variable rate loans. Variable rate loans are priced off the official interest rate, set by the Reserve Bank. They go up and down, but the home lending market is pretty competitive so you can look for the cheapest rate on the market. Fixed rates are set by the capital markets, off long-term bond rates. When you take a five-year fixed rate loan, you're betting that over the five-year period the variable rate will average more than the five-year mortgage rate. The banks' money market dealers have already factored in any advantage for themselves so why would amateurs like us feel that we can forecast five years of interest rates?

If you must use a fixed rate loan, do it for payment certainty, not for price. You might use it if, for example, you have an investment property and decide to pay back the interest on your mortgage, rather than both interest and principal. Taking out a fixed rate loan might help you match your incomings (rent) with your outgoings (interest) with some certainty.

won't understand how it really works until you throw yourself in.

We hear a lot of second-guessing when it comes to property: people say 'interest rates are going up so I'm not going to buy'. Or they say 'house prices are volatile so I'm not going to buy'. This would be fine if they were putting additional money aside so they could afford a better deposit when the time is right. But they usually don't.

Let me give an insight on this matter. First, over any ten-year period the value of the housing market always increases; you can find this information online at places like the Australian Bureau of Statistics and the Treasury. Second, when interest rates are low, the housing market is at its strongest—prices go up and the developers are building. Third, when interest rates are rising, the housing market cools and prices drop or stabilise.

So while you sit on the sidelines, rightly pointing out that there's movement and some uncertainty about where rates and prices will even out, you're overlooking one huge point: the housing market never stays still. Interest rates are always in flux, house prices are always changing, immigration keeps demand growing, and developers will keep supplying new places to live. Supply and demand are not perfectly matched, so there's always a closing or broadening gap between supply and demand. Buying such a large asset as a house is always going to be tough. It was tough when I bought my first apartment, and anyone else will tell you the same story.

The real problem that exists for first-time home buyers is not that the main indicators will fluctuate—of course they will. The real problem is that so many people have been trained to see property as a short-term investment. So when they see volatility in interest rates or prices, they get spooked. Perhaps we can blame the newspapers and promoters, but people really need to have their minds in the right place when they buy property.

Property is for at least ten years

Get this fact in your head and don't let anyone panic you out of it. To illustrate the dynamic nature of this market, consider these facts from BBB Capital (a Sydney investment bank and fund manager that I run with my two partners): the performance of residential property in 20-year chunks reveals that in the last 20 years, Australian residential property has made an average 12.1 per cent per annum (before tax and other costs). The key point to look at in this research is that the property market peaks on average once a decade (early 1960s, early 70s, early 80s, early 90s, early 2000s) and that each of these discrete property decades contains a two- to four-year period of price stagnation or decline. This is why you have to look at property in at least a ten-year framework—it allows all those competing market forces to do their thing and then be balanced by other forces. Imagine if you bought just before a period of stagnation or decline, and you were thinking short term. You'd sell. You'd miss the rebound to the peak. And you'd lose money and would probably not go into property again.

Here are some further perspectives on property that you may not have considered:

1 All mortgage lenders have factored at least three, and perhaps four, rate rises into your variable rate mortgage before they agree to provide the loan. So when the media does scare stories on the latest rate rise, you have to stay calm and realise that you'll just have to find slightly more money each repayment period. You're not alone, so don't take it personally.
2 The swings and roundabouts theory works very well on the property market: if you sit and wait for interest rates to go down, you'll find that property prices start picking up; if you wait for property prices to flatten out, you'll be in the middle of an interest rate rise. My rule for this is simple: *no-one outsmarts the market, so don't try!*
3 Selling in a falling market is the worst time to sell (it's the same for shares, by the way), as you get less money than you should. Evaluating your purchase after ten

years is the right way to go about this. Ideally, don't sell. Ever. It's better to use this asset to borrow against your equity than to sell the whole thing.

4 Demographics dictates all markets. It's especially true for property. Humans need food, shelter and water. The more people, the greater the demand for that finite resource of dwellings. The Australian government forecasts our population as growing at about 1 per cent every year until 2050. Most of the population growth will be driven by immigration—adults, with money, wanting to buy a house—and it will be in the large cities on the east coast of the continent; that is, Brisbane, Sydney and Melbourne and the satellite cities such as Newcastle, Wollongong and the Gold Coast. These places will increase by well over the average of 1 per cent, because they're getting net migration. Townsville, for instance, is forecasting population growth of 2 per cent per annum till 2026.

To sum up, you'll need an unencumbered place to live in retirement. And you'll be that much more comfortable if you have an income-producing property too. You have to start somewhere.

Building a property portfolio

In all the investments you make in an effort to increase your long-term income, you need to look for two things: income and growth. Income is the money that you receive from your investments. It's the payment you get for having your capital committed. With shares, your income comes from dividends, which may be between zero and 8 per cent of your holding. In property, the income component of your investment is the rental yield: 4.5 to 5 per cent per year for commercial property and 5 to 8 per cent for residential property. The residential yield, on average, should grow by about 5 per cent per year and capital growth should be about 8 per cent.

Income is one of the first things you must look for when you invest. You should be able to express the value of the income you receive as a percentage of what you paid for the investment. For example, if you paid $500,000 for an investment unit and receive $30,000 in rent, then your 'yield' before tax and costs is 6 per cent. 'Total return' would be the income you receive and the increase (or decrease) in the capital value of your unit. If the value increased to $525,000 in a year (5 per cent), your total return would be 11 per cent (income of 6 per cent plus capital gains of 5 per cent). These are the numbers you should be thinking about when deciding whether to buy an investment unit. The safe alternative—investing in a cash management trust—is very unlikely to provide an 11 per cent return.

But there's another thing: taxes and fees. When you buy an investment property, you get tax deductions on the interest payments you make and other costs like water rates and real estate management fees. But you pay tax on the rental income. And you'll have to pay tax on any capital gain you've made if you decide to sell the investment unit in the future. It's not a simple calculation.

A proper growth investment should be creating both income and capital growth. Whether shares or property or a business, your investment must be growing in value over time. If you're putting rent straight back into a mortgage or reinvesting share dividends (buying more of the same shares), you're increasing the capital you have invested. But it doesn't necessarily mean you're getting capital growth. Capital growth means the actual increase in value of the underlying asset. The value has increased, so the capital you've invested has increased. Hence, capital growth.

Property is one of those investments that can generate capital growth. The REIA figures show median house prices at $80,800 in 1986 and $396,400 in 2006.

A property strategy works like this: a well-bought property will generate income from rent and it can generate capital growth from the effects of time, inflation and market movements. That is, if you buy a property tomorrow, keep it for ten years and then sell it, you should have made money on the deal. At the very least, you should have matched inflation. In the Australian property market between 1992 and 2002, $100,000 invested at the start of that decade was worth $316,150 by the end. This is capital growth.

The Australian average for returns on residential property has been around 12 per cent per year in recent times, which is before taxes, fees and maintenance and repair costs. The return is a combination of capital growth and yield.

But how do you get income and capital growth from your family home? You live in it, which gives you security, and you pay a mortgage to the lender. No-one is paying rent to *you*. Where is the income in your capital?

The answer is that you must work towards buying another property which will provide you rental income. When you have this additional property you can truthfully claim that you have a property investment that produces income and capital growth.

How you get there is via equity.

Equity

Equity is the part of the house (or other asset, e.g. a company) that you own. It is essentially the value of the house, minus what you owe to the lender. So if you have a house valued at $1 million and you owe $500,000 to the bank, your equity is 50 per cent, or $500,000. If you sold the place, the equity is what you'd have left over after you settled with your lender.

So equity is very valuable. Yet most people sit on it. They let it build up over the years so that by the time they're in their forties or fifties, they have 50 or 60 or 70 per cent equity in their main family home. Sometimes they have 100 per cent, and it's just sitting there.

This can be a mistake. You can borrow against equity and use it as a deposit on an investment property or a share portfolio. It has a value when you find a lender prepared to help you 'leverage' your equity to buy something else. For now, let's look at how you can boost your equity.

Equity is created in two ways:

1 Capital growth
2 Reducing loan principal.

Equity builds up when the property market is going up and the property you own is in demand. You may also have done renovations which add to the value of the home. This increases equity because the mortgage stays basically the same but the value of the home increases, and that increases the equity you have in your home.

The other way that equity builds is via your repayment strategy. I've always thought that repayment strategies for homeowners are the most basic and accessible wealth-creation exercises available. They operate on the basis that all mortgages calculate interest on your loan on a daily basis and charge it to the mortgage every month. So if you have a monthly repayment schedule, the interest builds against you for a month and on the day you make your repayment, it pays that lump of interest before it goes anywhere else. This is the case for people (and that's most people) who have principal and interest (P&I) loans. Some of your repayment goes to pay down the principal of the loan—which is a good idea—and the rest chips away at the interest. That's why for most people it takes more than five years to start reducing the principal amount owing on the mortgage. You can't get going on paying down the principal amount of the loan because you're servicing this interest, which is constantly compounding against you.

One of the best ways to build equity in your property is to readjust the way you pay the mortgage, so that the repayments knock down the interest before it can compound too much. When you do this the repayments are working for you, not against you.

There are three ways they work.

1 Weekly and fortnightly repayments

If you have a standard variable rate loan, you can change from monthly repayments to weekly or fortnightly. This means the interest component of the loan does not compound against you as fast as when you pay monthly. It just can't accumulate to the same size because it's being knocked down at least four times a month (or at least twice a month for fortnightly repayments). Because there's less interest to pay off in a weekly repayment, your repayments pay off more of the principal. You get ahead of the compounding interest, the principal amount of the loan starts to reduce, and your equity grows.

On a $300,000 loan over 25 years at an interest rate of 6.71 per cent, paying fortnightly rather than monthly saves you $68,217.47 and reduces the loan term by four years and five months.

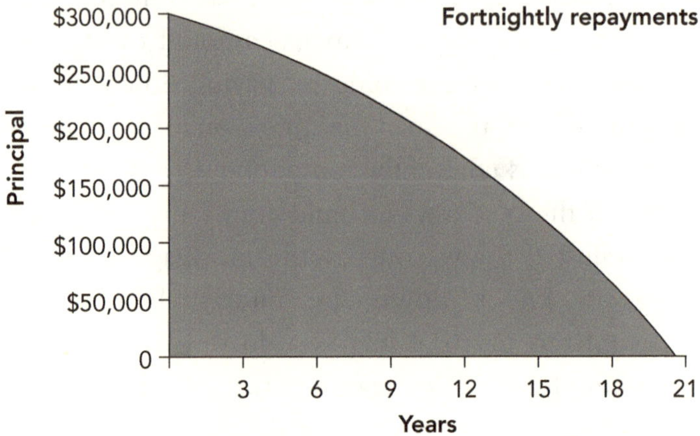

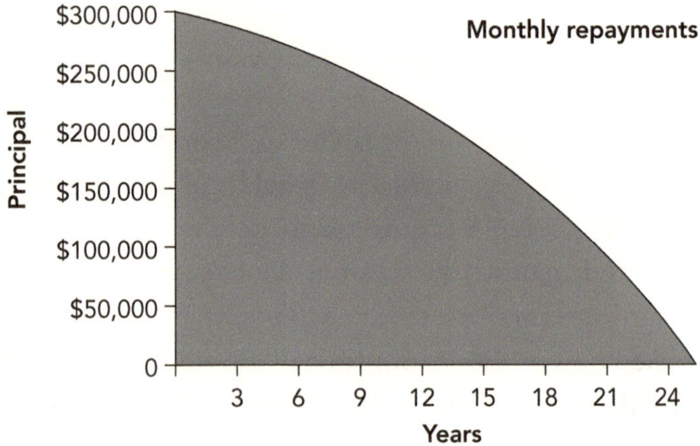

Source: www.wizard.com.au

2 Extra repayments

Even an extra $20 or $30 per mortgage payment accelerates the reduction of the principal amount of the loan. These extra payments go directly against the mortgage balance. As the principal starts reducing each month, the interest payments fall and you're building equity in your home.

On a $300,000 loan over 25 years at an interest rate of 6.71 per cent, paying an extra $30 in each fortnightly

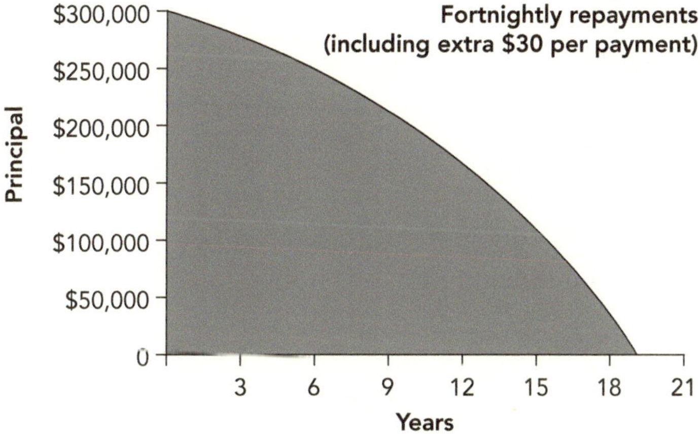

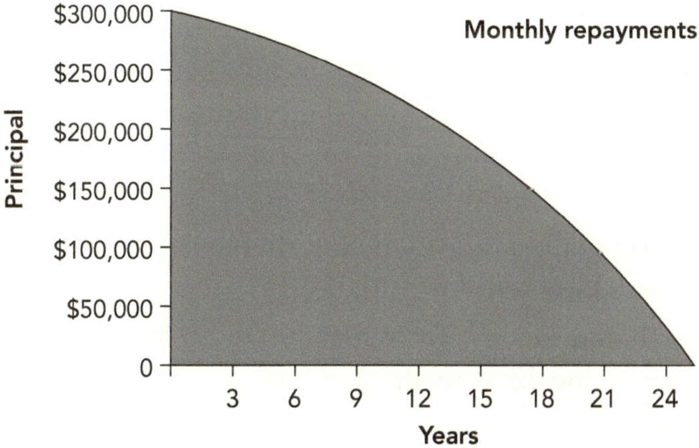

Source: www.wizard.com.au

payment saves $85,238.27 and reduces the loan term by five years and eight months.

3 Lump sums

From time to time you or a partner will get lump sums. It might be a tax refund cheque, an inheritance windfall, workers comp or a bonus from work. If you want to pay off your house quickly, the best place for lump sums, especially when your equity is down at the 10 or 15 per cent mark, is in your mortgage. Even modest lump sums can make a large difference in how fast you pay off your mortgage and the amount of interest you pay. And it will help you build equity in your home.

Leveraging the equity

Once you have more than 40 per cent equity in your main property, it's time to think about how to convert this into an income-producing asset—and doing so without challenging our golden rule that *we don't sell property*.

As I said in the passages above, in order to have properly performing assets in retirement you need to put your working years' income into assets that create capital growth and income for when you're no longer working. So what you have to do is create two properties where you previously had one, derive rental from one of them, live in the other, and get capital growth from both. And of course you want to have paid them both off by the time you retire.

Complicated? Not really. The point we start at is an understanding of how security works in the lending game. Security is what the bank can claim in the event that you don't pay your debts. Equity in a residential property is recognised as security—in fact it's the main security in small business lending and it's the security that the lender holds when they lend you the money to buy your house (which is why lenders prefer you have at least 20 per cent equity when you buy a house). Equity is also a valuable item to the lenders—so valuable that you can use equity in one property as security in another.

There are two ways you can do this: equity as deposit and cross-collateralisation.

Equity as deposit

If you take the value of your house and subtract the amount you owe on it (your mortgage) you have calculated the equity you have in your house. If you have built up equity over a few years, you can use it as a deposit for another property.

You are borrowing more money, using the equity in your house as collateral. This money is lent at your mortgage rate, which is comparatively low, and effectively means you don't have to save the deposit for another property purchase. This is a highly popular way of buying an investment property.

Cross-collateralisation

Cross-collateralisation is slightly more complex but also highly effective. You'll need to demonstrate to your lender your current position and income with the house you already own and the property you want. The lender will put the current property and the investment property you want to buy together on a single balance sheet. The combined value of the two properties becomes one amount; so does the equity and so does the mortgage. So if you have a $600,000 home with $300,000 owing, you have $300,000 equity, or 50 per cent. If you also want to buy a $300,000 investment property, the lender in this case would make it a $600,000 mortgage on property worth $900,000, with $300,000—about one-third—as equity. One-third equity is not bad. It's not enormous debt compared to your equity and still leaves you with options to buy again in a few years, depending on how fast you build up the overall equity. This is how most people build property portfolios for retirement, and they don't have to sell to do it.

However, you're still left with a large mortgage, which is why you have to get these strategies happening in your working years. Remember: it doesn't matter how sexy these deals look on paper, the lender will always assess you on your ability to repay the loan. It's called a 'debt-serviceability ratio'—your ability to service the debt. So we come round in a circle, back to income. Which is what we were chasing in the first place.

Generating income

Once you've used one of these equity-leveraging techniques you not only have a second property but you have a source of income from rent. During your asset-building years you don't need to live on this income, so you can put it straight back into your rental properties. In some cases, the rental income may come close to paying the mortgage payments; in other cases there'll be a shortfall which you will be able to claim as a tax loss in your income tax return (it's called 'negative gearing'—have an accountant or solicitor set this up properly). The point is, whether it covers the mortgage repayments and maintenance costs of being a landlord, or whether it's slightly short, the rental income is making it easier to own this investment property. And as the value of the properties grow, your equity grows too. And when this happens, you can borrow to buy more property or you can use the equity to diversify into a share portfolio. Or you can allow the repayments to build the equity and pay off the mortgages. Why? Because unencumbered property is what we really need for retirement.

Beware tax

Another thing to remember with investment properties is that if you ever want to sell one, it won't attract the concessional capital gains tax treatment that you have with your primary residence. Generally speaking the increase in the value of your family home is not taxable if and when you decide to sell it. But any increase in the value of an investment property attracts capital gains tax when you sell it.

I urge people who go into investment property to invest in a few hours with a financial adviser—an accountant, lawyer or knowledgeable financial planner—to have this properly explained and planned. There are issues here about the structure you use and the timing of buying and selling. Most of all, the disposal stage could easily land you with a high tax bill. This is often the case for couples who divorce and split the assets, or joint-owners where one of the owners wants to sell.

Buying an investment property

Many people buy investment properties on a hope and a prayer. They buy them because they can, because everyone else is buying them, because the sales brochures were so beautiful. My point in this book is to go back to what we're talking about for all investments: strategy, goal, discipline.

The same goes for investment properties. You may think what you're buying is a no-brainer, but what are you actually buying? Does it fit with your goals? Does it fit your strategy? Do you have the discipline to be good at this form of investing?

Let's start with the basics.

The best time to buy

As I write this we have just got to the tail-end of one of the biggest property booms this country has ever seen. In Sydney, Melbourne and Brisbane between 2001 and 2005 average house prices in some areas basically doubled. Even some rural prices have increased, despite the drought. Brisbane continues to boom and Melbourne is still doing okay. In Sydney the story is mixed. Perth's property market has taken off. But when the resources boom cools in Western Australia, Perth will see its own drop in property prices.

If you do what an increasing number of property investors are doing—judging property markets on three-, four- and five-year results—you'll never sleep at night and you should not be in the property investment world. Property is at least a ten-year investment. All the investment charts you see on the capital growth of residential property are tabulated in ten-year segments. This is because property is a high transactional cost investment to make. You need solicitors, you need property inspections, you need to pay stamp duty, loan establishment fees and land tax, and you need valuations done. So it's not like trading shares, where a stock price can go up in a week and the cost of trading is cheap.

There are also the factors that push property markets: property is enormously sensitive to basic household pressures such as interest rates, unemployment figures, inflation and consumer confidence in general. Australian residential property, at $2.1 trillion invested, is twice the size of the ASX capitalisation. And it's almost exclusively private ownership. So basic 'kitchen table' pressures like interest rates and inflation are what drive the whole thing. Therefore, property goes up and down all the time. But it always corrects. The REIA figures tell the story: for example, let's look at median house prices between 1986 and 2006. In the first decade, 1986–96, the median house price went down in one year, between 1990 and 1991. But in 1992 it rebounded to exceed 1990 levels. From 2004 to 2005, the median price dropped. But it rebounded in 2006 to exceed 2004 levels.

Once you understand this you'll realise that your entry into the investment property market should be made when you can. Don't try to time your entry with property—very few people outsmart property when it comes to timing. If you can afford it, go for it *now*.

Over any ten-year period you'll average a growth and income return of around 12.5 per cent. That equals about 7.5 per cent capital growth and 5 per cent rent (before tax and costs). But you won't get that every year—you have to be in it for the long haul to earn those averages. When I say 'Can you afford it?', I mean can you afford this investment over the ten years that property must be held as a minimum? For your interest, professional residential property investors are currently factoring an average interest rate of 8 per cent over ten years. That's how it works. Professionals don't make assumptions for a year or two years. When it comes to property, they're looking at no less than a decade.

Where to buy?

If I took the hypothetical case of where would I invest $500,000 right now, two ideas spring to mind. You either diversify and buy one $250,000 home in Newcastle and one in Mackay—both are 'second-tier' eastern seaboard locations with coastal residential areas. Or you go with the averages and assume that Sydney and Brisbane will have the biggest population growth over the next ten years, and therefore the highest growth in demand. In this case I would buy a house and land package in western Sydney from a good builder for $500,000.

These are two very different ideas and they both come out of my experience as an investor, developer and follower of market sentiment. Only experience can teach you some things, but following market sentiment tells you a whole lot besides.

Let's start with the second-tier markets. One reason you might look outside the major cities is that you get to buy more for your money in some of these places than you do in Sydney, Melbourne or Brisbane. But then again, you're unlikely to get the rental yield you want from some of the 'undiscovered' areas. You could be tempted to go for the cheap purchase in the untrendy town, but you're buying this property to rent, so you have to make sure you can get the steady rental income.

REDUCING RISKS IN THE PROPERTY MARKET

My own rule for selecting rental properties is as follows. I like newish properties, about two years old, constructed by a reputable builder. If it's an apartment, I search the body corporate minutes for complaints about kitchens, bathrooms and roofs, also cracking and uneven slabs—these are the main alarm bells. If a property has quality problems they will generally come out in the first two years.

As an overall rule, I like property near the coast, in a town or city with a population of more than 10,000, and near to good amenities. Is there a shopping centre or village nearby? Are there schools, churches and sporting clubs/facilities? It's also easy to find projections for the area on such things as net migration and new building approvals. Councils have all this information because they have to plan for areas to be developed and they have to put in infrastructure such as water and power. But you have to ask them for the projections, and sometimes in writing.

I also like areas that are within 100 km of an airport. In the 'undiscovered' places, I like to talk with real estate agents, builders and council people. Read the local rags. Get a feel for population growth and to what extent the council welcomes it. This gives me a sense of what will happen to rental yields. If I want to buy a property that's only returning 4 per cent rent (on house value), I have to form a view as to whether this will go up imminently. So I have to find out what yields have been like in this town, and whether incoming migration looks like it might outstrip new building. I have to form a view. So we're back to our basics of working out my income to support this, assessing the risk of the return, and capturing some sense of the market sentiment.

All in all, approach buying investment property as a natural extension of owning your own home. You have to select well, and buy well. The best laid plans come undone because you pay too much to start with and regret it later.

Managing a rental property

Once you own your investment property, you have to insure it, maintain it, lease it and manage the tenants. Some landlords get either a real estate firm or a leasing agency to do the work. Having someone else manage your property costs a percentage of the rental income, and frankly some of these managers are not worth the money. You can also self-manage, in which case the tenants deal directly with you and you check their references, employment details and rental histories, etc. By the way, always check these. It only takes an afternoon of phone calls and you might be surprised what you find. When you self-manage a rental property the idea is to have a tradesperson on call to deal with basics such as roofing and plumbing issues. If you lease the house as furnished or partly furnished, you'll want an appliances fixer too. You can do this when you have a property in another city as easily as when you have a rental property one suburb away from you. I suggest that when you first contact the maintenance person you leave a mobile number and don't tell them that you live in another city. Some people think they could or should charge you more or can get away with an inferior job if you live elsewhere. Don't give them the opportunity to push this style of business. You're also going to have to be a committed landlord. People are living in your property, and you have responsibilities to them. It's not for everyone. You have to decide where you sit on this—you can't be a part-time landlord.

You have to run your investment property like a business. This is why you can write off the costs of being the landlord: interest, depreciation, maintenance, management costs, etc. If the costs exceed the rental income, you can make this property a negatively geared venture—that is, your shortfall can be taken as a deduction against your assessable income, leaving you with a lower tax bill. First get advice from an accountant or solicitor on this.

Of course, I would encourage anyone buying an investment property to aim to have it making rather than losing money. I think you end up with a much better proposition by having to pay tax on money you're making than saving tax because you're losing money. The classic way people approach this is to have the property negatively geared during their working life—when the income tax reduction can help the most—with the goal of having the place making money from the rent when they retire and income from assets becomes the focus. If this is what you're doing, ensure that it's properly structured and planned. The last thing you need is a letter on the eve of your retirement from the Australian Tax Office demanding back taxes because you were claiming too much, or your property wasn't complying. I know that the Tax Office puts a lot of energy into its TaxPack, website and other user-friendly projects, but I am very, very cagey about do-it-yourself tax planning. The Tax Office people who put together all the PAYG documents for wage and salary earners are not the same people who do compliance testing and enforcement. If these people run a test on your numbers and decide you have been claiming too much for ten years, you'll be paying the lot back, with interest and potentially with penalty rates. And *then* you'll be using accountants and lawyers and financial advisers anyway, but there won't be a lot they can do except arrange an instalment agreement.

Preparing for retirement

One of the most interesting trends of the early 2000s has been a reversal of debt-retirement habits. Not so long ago, a couple in their fifties would be into the debt-reduction phase of their lives. In preparation for retirement—and with the kids out of the house—they'd be accelerating their mortgage repayments, putting lump sums into the mortgage accounts and trying not to get further into debt. But look at what former Reserve Bank Governor Ian Macfarlane said about this in a speech early in 2006: he noted that the fastest-growing group of borrowers in Australia were people in their late forties and fifties. I don't know where this trend will lead but it's a reverse of what used to happen.

Most of these people will be leveraging out the equity in their family home, in one of the ways I've listed above, in order to make sure they have enough income-producing assets in retirement. There are two observations I'll make about people doing this.

First, any real estate investment must have its own strategy and be part of a larger strategy. It has to be properly costed and not just a spur-of-the-moment thing that happened because someone at a barbecue, or a property promoter, told them to do it. If you're 55 and you reckon you can leverage the family home out to buy an investment property, and you can have that property paid off by the time you retire, then make sure it's properly planned. If you're expecting your superannuation payment will pay out the mortgage, then I would test this by making sure I had several different scenarios for how much super I'd get—most super funds have fluctuating returns and you may not get what you thought you would. My general warning to people is not to enter the retirement phase with debt hanging over them and with no Plan B. Debt is what you take on when you're out there earning income; debt has to be paid back.

My second point follows from this. Many of the older people taking on fresh debt when their forebears were getting rid of it are doing so through a facility called a 'reverse mortgage'. Essentially, a reverse mortgage is when you have an unencumbered house and a bank lends you up to 40 per cent of the value of it. The bonus is this: you stay living in the house and you don't have to pay the interest on this mortgage. Of course, there is interest—it capitalises in the loan account and balloons because no-one is paying the interest charge. It compounds at the market interest rate in the same way that money in savings compounds. When the reverse mortgagee dies or sells the property, the lender gets paid what they're owed. There are cases where people feel that this is the only option they could take—they say their super was not enough to live on yet they had this property worth $1.3 million. In effect, their property was the super. But I don't like the concept of reverse mortgage. The owners of those unencumbered properties have worked hard to own them and they could have been doing so much more with the equity than they obviously have, as I've already described. I also suggest that retirees or pre-retirees should think really hard about taking on debt at this time. Your retirement is supposed to be fun—who wants to worry about debt and interest rates? So downsize! If you decide that your only choice is to do a reverse mortgage, I would suggest that you first have a look at the real alternative: to sell the family home and move into somewhere cheaper and also unencumbered. Let's use the $1.3 million example again. You sell the house—free of capital gains tax—and buy a place to live in for $600,000. Then you either put the $700,000 into your super, or into a managed fund earning 8 per cent, or you buy an investment property which should yield on average 5 per cent per annum (without capital growth). The thing about downsizing your home is that you can stay unencumbered. Remember: there are always alternatives. You just have to find what they are.

Having a property portfolio of at least two assets is, I think, ideal for a happy retirement. You use the income from your working years to build equity via capital growth in your home, then you use that equity to buy another property that will produce income. If you time it right, in retirement you'll have a debt-free house to live in and a house producing income—with not a cent to pay in mortgage and with both properties continuing to produce capital growth.

I have shown you the bare bones of the property strategy. And, as with all things, having the goal and the strategy is only the beginning—then you have to throw loads of discipline at it too. But getting the discipline going, and buying a second property, opens up other issues, because once you become an investor you have to think more about yields. And this means you'll have to think more about what I call 'getting more yield out of the yield'. It requires professional advice from accountants or solicitors who are experts in tax.

The secret revealed

What you have just read is the so-called 'secret' to owning lots of properties fairly quickly (well, that's what the get-rich-quick promoters tell us). But as you can see there's no magic trick—it all comes back to working hard, having a plan and having the discipline to follow it through.

You need discipline to buy a property in the first place. It takes working, saving, perseverance and some faith, because at some point you're going to have to take that leap into a large asset with a large debt, then you'll have to keep working to create income so you can use an equity acceleration technique (I think you should use all three). And then you have to arrange your income and your borrowings again in order to buy an investment property. And once you have an investment property, you're a landlord and you now have a whole new layer of costs and responsibilities.

It all takes discipline, time and hard work—there are no overnight success stories, no quick-fixes, in property. As I keep saying, all property investments must be measured in at least ten-year timeframes. This is the one and only 'secret' of successful property investors. They simply discipline themselves to measure their investment in ten-year cycles. You might be wondering about all those people who allegedly doubled their money in three years in Melbourne or Sydney residential property? There were a few stories like that, but those stories were the big exception. In the early 2000s there was a large and historic correction of the Australian urban residential property market, and some people made a lot of money simply by being lucky. But luck is not what you want to rely on when you're saving for retirement. So I suggest this: if you can create the discipline of seeing property in ten-year slots then you are less likely to panic and more likely to make money and build security for yourself in your retirement. If you can think like this, you'll at least be starting from where the professionals start.

5

SUPER

I am a late convert to superannuation. When I first heard about it, I didn't really think that it applied to me. It seemed slow, and controlled by people I'd never met. It seemed distant, and reliant on political processes. I felt it was overly invested in another thing I didn't feel close to: the share market. It also seemed to be the boring way to create wealth—I was focused on my career, deals and income. Super seemed so far away and irrelevant.

I have changed this outlook. I now see superannuation as a very good, tax-effective way to save money and build income-producing assets for retirement. By combining professional investment managers, regular contributions and the compound effects of reinvesting returns, it's a powerful way to make sure there's a core of income-producing assets when you no longer work for your income. Best of all, it's a system accessible to all Australians: 9 per cent of our wages and salary has to be put into a complying super fund and then we get to choose which funds the money is invested in. And that money—averaged across all superannuation funds—has been producing returns of about 7 per cent per annum, although during the last four years the returns were better than 11 per cent.

Super is good for this country. Our system—the Superannuation Guarantee—means that taxpayers won't be slugged so hard to support an age pension in those years when there are too many retired people to be supported by a dwindling ratio of working-age people. By 2047 the proportion of the population under fifteen will decrease from what it is now, while the proportion and numbers of people over 65 will more than double. The proportion of the population who are working age (15–65) will stay much the same. It doesn't matter if you see this as the result of better life expectancy or lower fertility rates; the same proportion of working people will not be able to sustain double the number of elderly who want pensions. Those working-age people will be flat out paying taxes to fund the increasing public health bill.

It's not so simple as just telling employers to put 9 per cent of wages into super funds. Superannuation is a defined-contribution, or accumulation, scheme. And this puts the onus on the individual. So it's you who must select the best fund for your circumstances and take an interest in what your retirement savings are worth, whether you're accumulating at the right pace and whether those accumulations will be sufficient to fund a retirement you want. It's good in this respect. But it puts responsibility into the hands of people who may not feel qualified to have that burden. It creates opportunities and decisions that many people may feel are beyond their understanding.

At the same time, we live in a liberal capitalist society, and I think it's imperative that people being forced to save for retirement should be able to select an investment strategy suited to their financial goals. If they're risk averse, they should be allowed to choose lower annual returns in order to have stability and predictability in their returns. People who are aggressive should be allowed to receive higher returns as a trade-off for taking more risk and enduring greater volatility with their super. These are just some of the ideas we have to balance.

Yes, Australia's super system is a great idea: it has more than $1 trillion under management, which is increasing at about 15 per cent each year and is one of the best examples of its kind in the world. But there are issues, and the decisions that individuals have to make can mean the difference in hundreds and thousands of dollars in their retirement balance in 20 or 30 years' time. This is the part of super I think Australians should think more about and understand; the practical things like how you get money into super, how you get it out, what it does while it's in there, and what you can do to make sure that the money you need is the money you're going to get when you retire.

In 2005, 57.7 per cent of all superannuation assets were held in a fund's 'default' option. That means that well over half of all Australian workers have left their superannuation in the investment option chosen by their employer. That situation probably hasn't changed too much since then.

Some people may believe the default option is the best for them. But many would not have even bothered to think about it. Yet for many Australians, these could be some of the most important issues they confront in the second half of their lives.

It's time to build some basic understanding of super.

Super: the industry

Superannuation has not always been the universal, government-mandated, employer-supplied system that it is today. In 1985 only 39 per cent of the workforce had access to the tax-friendly investments of super, largely because it was limited to full-time corporate and public service employees, and was not generally available to blue-collar, casual (often female) employees. Until the early 1980s, just 24 per cent of women and 50 per cent of men had super savings. These were also the days of the defined-benefit schemes. As I mentioned in Chapter 1, defined-benefit super was calculated on receiving a benefit on a certain date, which could be boosted by voluntarily putting in more of your own money. Because of the way it was structured it favoured long-term, male, white-collar employees, and basically disregarded the rest.

The trade union movement agitated for a better system and in 1986 the Australian Industrial Relations Commission ruled that workers under an award would have an additional 3 per cent of their wages paid into super by their employers in lieu of a wage rise. In 1992 the government legislated the Superannuation Guarantee, which meant anyone earning more than $450 a month had an extra 3 per cent of their wage placed into super in lieu of a wage rise. This rose gradually for the next decade until it became 9 per cent in 2002. More than 90 per cent of Australian workers are now covered by the Superannuation Guarantee. In 2005 the government introduced Super Choice, so that employees could elect to send their SG payments to the fund of their choice. In 2006 the government radically changed the taxation of super to encourage people to save more for their retirement. Employer contributions are now taxed on the way in at a concessional rate of 15 per cent, and earnings in the superannuation funds are also taxed at a maximum rate of 15 per cent. Normally wages and investment earnings are taxed at a person's marginal tax rate (anything from 15 to 45 per cent). At the other end, benefits paid to retirees are now virtually tax free.

Managed funds

When governments mandate that 9 per cent of your wages must be transferred to the superannuation account of your choosing each quarter, you have the makings of a very powerful and very large industry. Managed funds have been around for more than 20 years, but the Superannuation Guarantee was a significant boost for the industry. There are hundreds of large superannuation entities, and more than 300,000 of the do-it-yourself funds with fewer than five members.

You should know a bit about what these large superannuation funds do and who they claim to represent. They are set up as trusts, administered by a board of trustees which generally appoints an asset manager to make investment decisions. Generally the fund buys and sells shares, bonds, cash, property and holdings in large infrastructure projects. Normally (but not always) the value of the fund increases, and so do benefits for members. The system is regulated by the Australian Prudential Regulation Authority (APRA) and the Australian Securities and Investments Commission (ASIC). Asset managers answer to the trustees, who answer to APRA and to members, who are people like us.

In the middle of 2007, total superannuation assets passed $1 trillion. The money was divided into five basic types of superannuation funds.

Retail

These large funds are run by household names such as AMP, BT and AXA, which have life insurance and bank origins. Each of these managers will typically have as many as 60 funds offered through their investment 'platform'. Their funds range from low-risk cash and fixed-interest investments that produce predictable income, to high-risk, potentially high-return shares-based funds. Some of the funds they offer are multi-manager funds, where the manager uses the skills of other managers to provide greater diversification in their offerings. Retail funds are the largest type of fund—they hold almost one-third of total super assets.

Self-managed super funds (SMSFs)

These are small funds, often part of the financial planning of a small or family-owned business enterprise. They have fewer than five members and, with certain legal and accounting compliance issues taken care of, these funds can invest in pretty much anything they like so long as they can show a real, commercial return to the members and so long as they don't borrow to fund investments (super funds can't borrow money). SMSFs—also known as 'DIY funds'—usually have their funds invested in cash, property and managed funds. There are more than 300,000 of them, making them the most numerous of fund types. They account for a little less than one-quarter of total super assets.

Industry funds

In the 1980s and 1990s these were known as 'union funds'. They covered an industry and gave workers access to basic fund types, such as property trusts, balanced, dynamic growth and fixed interest. Most are now 'public offer', and are open to anyone. They typically have fewer investment options than the retail funds—between ten and 20. The big selling point of industry funds is that they have lower fees, and few if any commissions paid by the funds to financial planners or other advisers. Industry funds generally offer full fund-administered life insurance and TPD (total and permanent disability) insurance cover. Industry funds may also offer low-cost banking and home loans through their own bank, Members Equity, and have discount buying schemes. Industry funds hold around 17 per cent of total superannuation assets.

Public sector funds

These are essentially the public service version of industry funds, except that a good proportion of the public sector funds are still defined-benefit schemes, such as the Public Service Superannuation Scheme (PSS). The PSS allows the employee to elect their contribution (from 2 per cent to 10 per cent), and that contribution is matched by the employer. The payout is devised by reference to final salary and time in the job. There are other public sector funds that run like industry funds and they are accumulation schemes. Whether you're in a defined-benefit or accumulation scheme is largely based on when you joined the organisation. The accumulation schemes perform at a similar level to industry funds, although they tend to have more money in life insurance products than do the industry funds. Like industry funds, public sector funds also hold about 17 per cent of super assets.

Corporate funds

Some companies retain their own super funds, with employees and owners as the members, and usually management and some senior staff as the trustees. They outsource a lot of their funds management functions to expert service providers such as asset advisers, auditors, assurance and compliance people, economists and fund managers. So they have as much expertise working for them as any large fund, even though they may have as few as five or six investment options. They also have tended to perform as well if not better than retail funds, according to APRA. They make up around 6 per cent of total super assets in Australia.

What do super funds do?

Superannuation funds invest super contributions from employers and members and, hopefully, boost retirement incomes. They invest in bank accounts. They invest in government and company bonds—a type of IOU—whereby they receive regular interest payments. They invest in share markets in Australia and overseas, where they earn money from share prices rising (capital gain) and dividends (income). They also invest in what's known as 'alternative investments'. These include private equity, some property deals and other, more sophisticated products. During the accumulation years, the returns are ploughed straight back into the members' accounts, which creates the magic of compound earnings (see box on page 107). Only, in the super system, you have a further boost to the compound scenario by having regular Superannuation Guarantee payments put into your super account by your employer. And if you're really smart, you're putting extra from your salary into super by way of salary sacrifice, which for many medium-income earners creates a tax advantage as well. The concessional tax treatment of superannuation also helps the compound magic along: the tax on earnings in super funds is a maximum of 15 per cent, as opposed to the marginal tax rate you pay on earnings from investing in shares or a managed fund. So your money compounds faster in super than it can when you personally invest your after-tax dollars.

In order to make these returns, trustees of funds create investment options within a super fund. This allows investors who have already established their goals, strategy, risk profile and diversification needs to decide how they want their money invested. Options might include local and global property funds, local and global equities funds, or local and global cash and fixed-interest funds. Some funds might have options that invest in small companies or 'emerging markets'; some options invest in ethical stocks and some invest in market indices that replicate what's happening in the share market.

While some people are in the accumulation phase of their super and are focused on assets that deliver capital

THE MAGIC OF COMPOUNDING INTEREST

If you're putting off saving for retirement, you need to know about compounding interest. It's the main reason why people who start putting money away when they're young end up so much better off in their retirement years. Compounding interest refers to the fact that if you reinvest interest payments each year (rather than spending them), you will earn interest on both the principal amount and on the previous year's interest. Let's say you invest $1000 in year one and earn 10 per cent ($100) on it. In year two, assuming you have reinvested everything and you once again earn 10 per cent, you will receive interest of $110. Following the same pattern means that after a little more than seven years, you have doubled your money.

Now translate that into a $30,000 share portfolio. Let's say you invest $30,000 in shares and receive, on average, a return of 12 per cent each year. You reinvest all your returns. In 25 years' time, that share portfolio will be more than $500,000. And all you've done after your initial investment is let the magic of compounding interest work.

growth (like shares), others, usually in the retirement phase, are focused on how to get regular, stable income from theirs. This income phase is usually satisfied by the super funds' pension, annuity and income products: more on that later.

In all of the super fund product disclosure statement (PDS) documents, you can read what the funds do, find out what proportions of them are invested in which markets or sectors, and learn which risk profile is suited to a particular fund. The streams of information that pour out of the super fund industry are huge, so there's no excuse to not know what's going on.

Generally, the manager of a super fund will focus on four main types of asset.

1 **Shares:** This is the most price-volatile asset class, yet can also create the highest returns over the medium and long term and can provide tax-effective income. Ups and downs caused by industry or market or economic fluctuations can spook conservative investors. Some 'defensive' stocks create income with less volatility, but mostly investors are looking for capital growth with this class of asset and are willing to accept the volatility.
2 **Property:** The manager may invest in listed property trusts, property companies and property-related companies such as mortgage trusts. Mainly they are looking for rental yields but there should be capital growth too. More stable than shares and only slightly behind on performance.
3 **Fixed interests:** Fixed-interest securities are often in the form of bonds or other securities that represent an underlying loan to governments and corporations. They are highly stable—because there's a fixed amount of interest being paid on the loans—but they're also poten-

tially risky in terms of sudden rate rises and loan defaults. If the investment manager doesn't get it right, there's a chance that you could lose some of your capital.

4 **Cash:** Highly stable but low-returning. Cash refers to short-term, market-traded financial instruments issued by corporations and governments generally accessed by investors through cash management trusts. Your investment capital (what you put in) is quite secure, but after tax and inflation you may earn a negative return.

In the 'balanced' funds, you'll see all of these mixed together, in different ratios depending on the risk profile and term of investor.

By now, you should be getting a good idea of where you want to be and what mix you want.

Trustee and manager expertise

You could ask yourself why you wouldn't just manage your superannuation investment, given that many of the investment managers follow market indices such as S&P/ASX 200 or the All Ordinaries Index on the Australian Stock Exchange. The answer is the number of techniques employed by the professionals which you would never do yourself.

Let's start with the most obvious reason for leaving this to a professional: you have to at least beat inflation. This is an often-overlooked and untrendy point, and one that

I seem to focus on in a rather lonely way. The truth about money and wealth is that it shrinks every year. It discounts by the inflation rate, which recently has been between 2 and 3 per cent. So if you had $100 today, you'd need $134 in ten years' time in order for it to have the same buying power. The personal finance media don't write much about the inflation risk, but the professionals do think about it. (If you don't think about the effects of inflation, it's good to know that the professionals do. It's their job.)

There's also risk/return balance, which can be difficult to establish and even harder to maintain. Professional managers are very good at creating easy-access products. I covered this in Chapter 1, but let's look at it again. Money you invest earns larger returns if you take a greater risk. And in order to enjoy the long-term higher returns of this greater risk, you have to be invested for a longer time. There are investors who want certainty and liquidity in their retirement savings, and are prepared to take the lower returns for this risk averse view. And there are investors who want their money working for them for 20 to 30 years, and are prepared to use this time-frame to weather the volatility of higher-risk investments in order to get the higher returns in the long term. And you can imagine how many points there are in between.

What the fund management professionals do is create investment products where non-professionals can elect an investment style and risk/return profile that suits their strategy. This is why I believe that all Australians have to know their goals and understand their strategy, regardless of who actually executes the plan.

Some of the fund managers offer up to 90 different investments, with every life stage and risk profile and return 'appetite' catered for. The funds are generally made up of the four classes: shares, property, fixed interest and cash.

There are other investments, called 'alternatives', and they cover private equity, venture capital, derivatives, hedge funds and futures, commodities and other products. The media makes quite a bit of these because they sound sexy and the returns—in recent years often topping 15 per cent—are alluring. But mostly these investments are offered by managers through wholesale funds, and they will only accept the investment via advisers and from 'sophisticated investors'. More about advisers and planners later.

Investment managers say they offer other specialised services, although you always pay for it. They employ a whole lot of financial market techniques that they claim will boost your chance of making money and reduce your chance of losing it. These techniques include a range of 'hedging' strategies, active currency management, interest rate strategies, forward foreign exchange contracts, short selling (they use specialist funds to do it), and hybrid securities strategies. Certainly these aren't things that most individuals understand—they are very specialised. If you are investing personally and want to get involved in such exotic investments, you must make sure you know where you're putting your money. And remember that there's always a potential downside to these exotic investments. If you want to invest in them, use the experts. But go in with your eyes wide open, realising that there are never ever any guarantees when you invest in financial markets.

Advantages of super funds

Let's say you have your money in a share portfolio or a plain managed fund. Every return you make from these investments is taxed as personal income. That is, if you make a return of $10,000 from a managed fund, that $10,000 is simply loaded on top of your taxable salary and the new total is what you're taxed on. The income from your managed fund is taxed at your top personal marginal tax rate, plus the Medicare levy. Of course you might earn some franking credits, thereby lowering your tax bill. Franking credits in Australia (also known as imputation credits) were introduced in 1987 to stop double taxing of company earnings. Companies that pay tax on their earnings can distribute 'fully franked' or 'partly franked' dividends to shareholders. The idea is that the company has already paid tax on the money that is used to pay dividends, so the shareholder shouldn't have to also pay tax. The shareholder receives a franking credit which they can use to lower their tax bill.

Compare the tax on a share portfolio with a superannuation fund: annual returns earned by super funds are taxed at a maximum rate of 15 per cent.

Another cost-saving and life-enhancing feature of super funds is the cheap—or at least tax-effective—insurance. If your super plan has insurance cover it will generally offer life insurance and total and permanent disability insurance. This can be very useful, especially for people with kids. When you're in the right super fund, you pay your premiums from your super which is pre-tax money. Generally, this is a cheaper, more tax-effective way of having insurance than paying the premiums out of your pocket from post-tax income. I also urge anyone who values their income-producing abilities to cover themselves for the eventuality of being injured or sick and being unable to work for a few months. That means taking out income protection insurance.

I would also have a look at the co-contribution scheme: if you earn less than $58,000 a year, you can make personal contributions to super and the government will match you up to $1.50 for every $1 you put in, depending on your earnings level. This is money for jam, and I urge people to at least think about it. The same goes for salary sacrificing extra super contributions. We've all been told that 9 per cent of salary is not going to be enough to retire on. There are tax benefits for most earners in making extra contributions from pre-tax salaries and wages. Get professional advice on this one.

When it comes time to retire and you want money to live on, superannuation has big advantages. If you have a share portfolio or a managed fund that you want to live on in retirement, the income you receive will be taxed like personal income. With super, you can take the money three ways: rollover into an allocated pension, rollover into an annuity product, or lump sum. None of these attract any tax if you're over 60 years of age. You can even partake in a tax-friendly scheme called 'transition to retirement': you draw down some of your tax-free super while you're still working, and contribute more of your wages to boost your super account. The money going into super attracts a 15 per cent contributions tax rather than the marginal tax rate you would pay on your wage.

These are big benefits, by the way. You can stay in your fund for life, with your investments being taxed at a 15 per cent tax rate, or you can take a tax-free pension. It's a definite advantage for people who want to be able to plan for life after work without having to worry about who'll subsequently manage their money. Either way, I reckon you win with super.

There's just one catch: you need enough in your super to live on.

Selecting a fund

Every super fund will be slightly different, but at the very least it has to be a fund that suits who you are and what you want to achieve. I urge you to have a look at the following list, and select a fund using these criteria:

- Accepts employer and salary sacrificed contributions
- Accepts personal contributions
- Accepts rollovers/transfers from other superannuation

funds, providing you with the ability to consolidate all your superannuation funds

- Offers you investment options you understand and are comfortable with
- Provides internet access so that you can view your superannuation online
- Includes the option of purchasing life and total and permanent disability insurance.

I'm not going to get too far into super fund performance in this book. They all change, all the time, for different reasons. Different funds have their moment in the sun, as do different fund managers, different industry sectors and fund types. What goes up usually comes down, and I'm not going to pick winners when the winners change from quarter to quarter.

What I can say is that there's so much material on superannuation funds that there's no excuse to not be informed about—at the very least—how your current fund is doing compared with others. You must know about the performance of this asset which will form the centre of your happy retirement. Your super fund will have a website, and that should be your first stop. And I suggest you look at sites such as:

- the federal government's Understanding Money website, www.understandingmoney.gov.au/content/default.asp
- APRA's website, www.apra.gov.au/Superannuation

- the Australian Bureau of Statistics (ABS) site, www.abs.gov.au/websitedbs/D3310114.nsf/home/home
- the Money Management site (where you can look at all Standard & Poor's listings of managed funds), www.moneymanagement.com.au/sp.asp
- the Morningstar rankings at www.morningstar.com.au.

The list is long, and to that I could add van Eyk, Intech, CommSec, ASSIRT and many more. The more you look around the more you'll find, and it's your job to read them, know what they mean for you, and keep looking at and perhaps slightly adjusting your strategy to meet your goals.

In general, government sites such as ABS and APRA will give broad performance in terms of superannuation and fund type. They let you know, for instance, that the industry funds have done better than retail funds in recent years, and that public sector funds have done better than both. These are 'macro' figures, and many people choose which fund they use based on this information.

The 'micro' performance of personal investments is better gauged from Standard & Poor's (S&P; through the Money Management site) or Morningstar, which also provides the daily fund performance numbers in the *Australian Financial Review* (*AFR*). These are my preferences. Here, individual managed funds are listed with their cost and a performance figure. The performance figure is expressed as a percentage return, over a certain period of time. It's important to look at the long-term average performance. That way you can check out how a managed fund is doing over a timeframe that's more likely to match your investment. You also need to consider the short term, because the fund manager may have done well in the past but not so well in more recent years.

Important also is the performance as it relates to costs and fees. In Australia, fund managers are required to declare their costs and fees by providing investors with an MER (management expense ratio) for each fund. It's expressed as a percentage. So an MER of 2 per cent means the manager is charging 2 per cent of the total funds under management. Whether you use S&P or *AFR*/Morningstar or some other measure, keep an eye on the MERs. The reported returns of a fund don't include the MER. Most rankings provide a benchmark for the average performance of a type of fund over different time periods. So you can easily test

PICK ONE AND STICK TO IT

One tip I got from one of my investment banker advisers is that it doesn't really matter which analyst or ratings expert you use, but once you've established who you're listening to you should stick with them. If you like the S&P charts, stick with them. If you're used to the *AFR*/Morningstar lists, stick with them. This way you'll always be comparing apples with apples. The fund ratings people all have slightly different ways of coming up with who's performing best. If you stick with one technique, you'll have more clarity.

if your personal investment is performing above or below the benchmark for the fund type, and also investigate how other funds are doing. The same type of benchmarking is promoted by super funds.

Of course, every person reading this will have a different type of fund they want to follow. This is why it's best to get your information straight from the *AFR*/Morningstar or S&P lists—you can browse and find what you're looking for, rather than have someone tell you what you should be finding. Get used to reading these charts and it becomes second nature.

Quartiles

If you're thinking of changing your fund because you don't like their performance, or you're changing your risk profile, or you want a bigger range of fund types, the chart you should be looking at is the 'quartiles' chart.

Quartiles are just what they sound like: Morningstar and other ratings agencies take all the funds in a certain segment of super funds and rank them into four bands based on returns. It's about the most easy-to-read peer comparison you can get in the financial markets.

'Second quartile' funds are running hard, but not so hard that they're bouncing from quartile to quartile like a yoyo. So if you want to follow quartile rankings, go to a site like Morningstar and dig deep. Find three-year quartile reports for the fund you're interested in. If it averages three quarters of each year in the second quartile—nine quarters out of

SECOND IS BEST

Another tip I picked up from professionals is this: when selecting a new fund, never pick the funds from the top quartile of performance—always pick from the second quartile. It doesn't sound right, does it? But all the pros I've spoken to say that the top quartile performers are only in the top quartile for one or two quarters of reporting, and then sink quickly to third or the bottom quartile. This happens because they're under pressure to continually outperform other funds, and if they have had a strong twelve months they need an even stronger year to keep outperforming and remain in the top quartile. This could trigger extra risk-taking.

twelve—then you're looking at a good performer with a stable investment performance relative to other funds; it has a sustainable way of achieving good returns. If you can't find the information, ask your planner or adviser—they may be pleasantly surprised that you don't want a top quartile fund.

Beating inflation

My simplest tip when it comes to fund performance is the issue of inflation. I try to remind people about this, but it's just not sexy. People with a natural bent towards conservative, low-risk investing inevitably slide further down the returns scale until they are invested mostly in the risk averse universe of fixed interest and cash. They think this is risk free. I don't agree.

As I said before, we've gone through a period of low inflation where investors, economists, bankers, business-people and fund managers have all been able to relax a little. But retirement investing is for the long term, and everyone should be aware that inflation goes up and down over the years. Three per cent is simply a long-term average. Inflation will come back and it will hurt people with a risk averse approach to super. It worries me a little. Sometimes the biggest risk is not taking enough risk. I won't be prescriptive about this—I don't have a crystal ball. What I will say is that every investor should think like the professionals and make their first test of any investment: Will it beat inflation?

In reality, the only way to judge a long-term investment like superannuation is to discount all returns for inflation. If you're in a fixed-interest fund returning a five-year average of 4.6 per cent, you've actually been making about 1.7 to 1.8 per cent. If you understand this and you're happy, that's great. But for most people this is not a sustainable long-term strategy.

Super retirement strategy

The simple job of your super account is to amass enough money that in your retirement it will pay you the amount of money you not only need, but want.

The whole strategy starts to come together: you need your unencumbered house to live in rent and mortgage free; you need a share portfolio as a fund for non-core living needs, such as gifts, holidays and helping out the kids; and you need your health to enjoy it all. (I think an investment property is a good idea too.)

But it's the super that sits in the middle and gives you your living money. This is the part of the overall strategy that's really crucial. Because of its tax-friendly nature and its 'untouchability', and because it's mandated by government, there's no reason not to have this as the dominant form of income-producing asset in retirement.

Let's assume your central income engine is super, without taxation complications. You can see without even reaching for a calculator what the sums start to look like: if you have $1 million in super, in a medium-risk fund returning about 7 per cent, you can cover the cost of living without gouging into the capital amount of your investment. That capital gets to sit there and be your slush fund for big holidays, loans to kids, paying for grandkids' education, etc.

However, what usually happens is that the retiree doesn't live off the pure distributions of their super: they buy an annuity product which provides regular income over a long period; those with comfortable savings may do their own calculations and create their own budgets for eating into their capital and paying themselves distributions. During the time that you're taking income from your super, it might be getting smaller as a total size, but the investments are still making earnings and they're still compounding. And you want to make sure you get it right so that you don't over-spend and under-provide.

In the real world, the majority of people don't have $1 million in their superannuation account. The problem, if you take the reports in the media and from government and industry associations as a guide, is that Australians have nowhere near enough in super to fund these basic levels of living in the future. APRA's report, *Insight: Celebrating 10 years of superannuation data collection 1996–2006*, which was released in mid-2007, reveals the truth about super: 'Corporate funds had an average account balance at the end of June 2006 of $86,500. Public sector funds had an average balance of $52,400 and retail funds had, on average, just $28,800 in each super account. But there's worse news. The average account balance in industry funds was just $15,100.'

It's obvious there's a major financial shortfall for most people wanting a comfortable retirement.

Funding the shortfall

Some super fund members still have a long time in which to save. For some retirees, part of their shortfall may be funded by selling the family home and downsizing to something more modest, and investing the balance as an income-generator. This is what generations of retirees have done previously. And this is one of the attractions of devoting yourself to the mortgage when you're in your income-earning years.

Others won't have to sell the family home because they have an investment property that produces income. Average rental yield for Australian residential property is 5 per cent, and it's taxed at your top marginal tax rate. If, in 2026, you have $2 million worth of investment property, producing $100,000 of rent per year, you'll still be taxed, but that will bring you down to around $63,000 (which is what $35,000 in today's dollars will then be worth).

Others sell off their share portfolio, or start to release the dividends to their bank account rather than letting them build in the portfolio. Again, this is an asset that was built during the income-producing years. Others may have to rely on whatever age pension is left.

The other way to fund the shortfall between needs and savings is to start on a top-up strategy years before you retire. For a number of years, reputable economists, actuaries, fund managers and trade unionists have been claiming that, in order to fund retirement properly, employees need to put 15 per cent of their salaries into super, not 9 per cent (the original plan for the Superannuation Guarantee was to have it progress to a mandated 15 per cent). I have no reason to believe that 15 per cent is not the optimum amount of wages to be put aside as super, but I can't see the Superannuation Guarantee rising to that level any time soon.

My approach in the meantime is that individuals will have to make up the shortfall themselves. You can do this by putting extra money into your super through salary sacrificing. This is a very tax-effective way to increase your savings, especially for people whose income is just above a tax bracket. If you earn only $2000 or $3000 over the cut-off for the 40 per cent marginal tax rate, for example, you can salary sacrifice this amount to super, which brings you under that tax threshold and essentially means that the tax saving is funding your super top-up.

The new super rules allow people to put $50,000 a year into super as a before-tax contribution, and up to $150,000 as an after-tax contribution. You can even put $450,000 into a super fund as a lump sum, and you're allowed to average it over three years. This is really good for business owners and people selling real estate. A business owner can sell a business at a capital gain, and if they put up to $500,000 of the sale price into super it's free of capital gains tax. That's a pretty massive saving, and one that can be drawn out of super at the other end without any tax.

It's also very good for men or women who may have received a lump sum such as a divorce settlement: if you still have a job, the extra money from the settlement is excellent value invested in a super fund. You receive it tax free, there's no contributions tax, and earnings are taxed at a maximum rate of 15 per cent. When you take it out in ten years' time, it's tax free. This of course assumes that you already have your house sorted out, which should be the first priority.

As you can see, there are ways to get extra money into your super without the government having to legislate your employer to do it. For those getting close to retirement, there's no reason why you shouldn't put all your money into super. It goes in, earns returns for a few years, and then you take it out tax free. If you have a share portfolio that has grown to a certain level, or you've grown tired of it, you might want to sell it and put the proceeds into your super fund.

How will I get it out?

When it comes to super and retirement strategies, every Australian should at some point talk with a professional. The Understanding Money initiative, which has a website and a budgeting and planning booklet, is a good start. Then, if at all possible, spend some time with a financial adviser. Recent changes to superannuation laws that encourage investment for retirement are worthy initiatives, particularly for older Australians. But I believe more needs to be done, especially for younger Australians. Perhaps the government could boost people's super accounts by providing a one-off boost to all super account members. It would be a great investment in the financial wellbeing of this country.

For now, perhaps the most confusing aspects of super—and retirement planning in general—are how to access your savings, how to make it go as far as you want it to, and how to balance meeting your financial needs and having enough money to live out a comfortable retirement.

In other words, if I think I'm going to pass away in 20 years, I can eat into my principal amount by, say, $4000 a year, as well as taking the returns as income. But what if

I live for 25 years? What if I only live fifteen years? Should I have been spending that principal amount faster? After all, I worked for that dough—shouldn't I have been enjoying it?

This, I'm afraid, is the unsexy stuff. It all sounds so exciting when you're talking about how fast your money grows with compounding and with low taxes and professional investment managers, but this 'back end' discussion is usually where even the most informed and diligent DIY investors are going to have to buy some expert advice.

Everyone about to go into this phase must see an adviser (one you're happy with) and at least have the issues and the options clarified. A few general points to remember:

- The age you can access your super is 55 and over (if no longer working full-time); 60 and over (if not working at all); or 65 and over (whether you work or not).
- You can take a lump sum and become a DIY retiree.
- You can 'rollover' the super into an income-stream product such as an allocated pension or an annuity.
- You can leave your money in your super fund and take out money when you need it.
- You can work out a strategy that combines some or all of the above options to maximise your retirement benefits.

Lump sum

Every Australian has the right to take their superannuation savings as a lump sum, and as of 1 July 2007 the whole amount is tax free. It doesn't get much simpler. Whether it's $100,000 or $1 million, you get the lot. But from here, you'd better have a plan and you'd better have good advice. I've already touched on some of the living and money issues for retirees, and when you take a lump sum the entire responsibility falls on your head. A popular way to invest a lump sum is to pay down debt—usually on share portfolios and property. These unencumbered assets now become your income engine for retirement. If you're already debt free, the lump sum buys more shares or more property, with probably a decent amount now sitting in cash. The idea here is that you simply convert all of that money that's been building up into income, such as property, which yields at 5 per cent; a conservative 'yielders' share portfolio, which should yield around 4 per cent and continue to grow; and some cash, which will return whatever the rate of the day happens to be.

Having already worked out what you'll need in retirement, you choose the best investment. The risks are that the share market will tank, and if you have no discipline you could easily be flustered into low-return investments (see Chapter 6 on having your own portfolio and in particular what I say about being disciplined). The rental market could also go flat and you may feel tempted to sell an investment property at the wrong time. These are market risks—the same risks you've taken during the accumulation phase. Now, you have 20 years or more to make it last and you might not be so calm about market fluctuations. You have to make an assessment about who you are and how relaxed you can be managing a lump sum for income.

Also the kicker is tax: your retirement income will be assessed under the personal income regime.

Allocated pension

An allocated pension is a product tailored to each investor. You put your superannuation money—or part of it—into one of these products and it produces a monthly income from the investment returns of the money you put into it. It's designed to both distribute returns and to eat away at the capital so that over a period of 20 or 25 years it runs down to zero. The benefits of this are that the capital amount is still invested and is still earning returns from the risk/return profile that you choose. These earnings are tax free and income paid to you is also tax free if you are 60 or over. Some people who have allocated pensions can also qualify for Centrelink payments. The drawbacks: the money is still 'actively' invested, and the returns—especially if invested in share funds—can be volatile.

Annuity

The annuity is similar to the allocated pension, except what you're buying is a life insurance-based product. The issuer sells you a package of a set amount of income, paid regularly, based on the amount you invest and your life expectancy. It's a fixed interest rate which goes for the life of the product, although it's usually adjusted for inflation. Few go beyond 25 years.

Annuity products and lump sum

Professional advisers can show you how taking a mix of your superannuation lump sum and an annuity-style income product leaves you better off in terms of tax, income and continued capital growth of your investment. People with enough in the tank when they retire can have these options. If your super is big enough, you can have your allocated pension product invested in a moderate fund and put the rest of your lump sum into a more dynamic investment. Or you can go on the dream holiday and buy the flash car.

To get the full benefit from your retirement savings you'll need an adviser who specialises in retirement planning. They can help you formulate a plan which will be best for you. It might combine lump sums, allocated pensions and annuities, or two of the three, or perhaps just one of the options. They might even be able to get you entitlement to a portion of the age pension.

Financial planners

No chapter on superannuation is complete without the subject of advisers, and for most people that's going to mean financial planners.

Throughout this book I've talked about the importance of having:

1 Goals
2 Strategy
3 Discipline.

All Australians should know what these are in terms of retirement planning. I also said you need to understand:

1 Income
2 Risk
3 Diversification
4 Market sentiment.

You probably don't have the technical expertise to rebalance your investments every year, create a new mix of assets based on your risk profile, and make sure the weightings in that portfolio reflect both your strategy and your need for risk-mitigation techniques such as diversification. Plus you need to appreciate the tax implications of all decisions you make.

It's complex, I agree. And because it's complex—and because super is the most tax-effective way to amass money and you might only get one chance to do it right—you'll need a professional to advise you. Who do you pick?

This has become a vexed topic in the last few years, largely because many financial planners are remunerated by the managed funds industry who want the financial planners to sell their products. This works in several ways.

Some planners earn an up-front commission from the managed fund for putting their clients into the fund. The commission is typically up to 4 per cent of the rollover balance. Many planners also earn a 'trailing commission', which is normally between 0.2 and 0.6 per cent of your balance while it stays in the fund, and it's paid monthly.

There are also planners who earn a commission and trailing commission for either selling you insurance, or earn a fee if they refer you to someone who does sell insurance products.

There's also 'soft-dollar' commissions: trips overseas for conferences, footy tickets, meals at nice restaurants paid for by the big financial institutions.

You can understand why planners don't want to give this up. In the case of trailing commissions, these notionally pay for your ongoing reviews—yet many planners do not automatically provide annual reviews and some charge additional fees.

This system can create a massive conflict for the planner, and a lack of transparency for the client. This is why ASIC and the Australian Consumers' Association have both come out against this form of remunerating planners. Both are worried about the kind of advice a person receives when the planner has a financial incentive to recommend a particular managed fund which may not be the best one for the client. Jeffrey Lucy, past chairman of ASIC, spoke at the Financial Planning Association conference in 2006, and this is what he said to them: 'The fundamental question an adviser must ask as they consider the interests of their clients and their own business needs is: whose side am I on?'

In the last few years, some financial planners have introduced much more transparent fee structures. Some have a 'fee for service', much as for a solicitor or accountant. It sounds good but there have been some problems, not least a large up-front cost faced by the investor. Also, planners who work for a large dealer network may be charging a fee for your service, which looks 'unbiased', but might be penalised in salary or bonuses for selling people the 'wrong' managed fund.

The next phase of remuneration is the one I like. It's called 'fee-based' financial planning. In fee-based financial planning, the adviser hands back as a rebate to the client all of the commission payable by the fund manager. Normally that rebate is reinvested into the client's portfolio.

The adviser charges a fee on a pre-arranged basis. Sometimes it will be a dollar figure. Other times it will be a set percentage of the total size of the portfolio. If you invest with a credible firm, the fee tends to reflect the services you get, but as a minimum you should ask for an annual consultation, ongoing portfolio management, regular rebalancing and online and phone access.

When looking for a planner, you should expect the following:

- Help with defining your long- and short-term financial and personal goals
- Clarification of your risk profile
- Superannuation advice, including what type of superannuation investment vehicle is best for you
- Investment advice and wealth-creation strategies, based on your needs and goals (not on theirs)

- Insights on some taxation and accounting matters
- Help with mortgage and personal debt-reduction strategies
- Guidance on life insurance and estate planning
- A savings plan for retirement
- Advice on government payments.

Finding a planner

But that still leaves you with the problem of how to find these people. Websites such as the Financial Planning Association and ASIC provide 'find a planner' searches. It's a good start to use these to see if there's someone in your area who fits some of the criteria you set yourself: it could be that you want a female adviser, or you want someone who understands small business issues, or someone who's experienced with self-managed super fund set-up and management. There's no harm asking your friends who they recommend. Of course, you can always come to my company, Yellow Brick Road, to find a good adviser!

Summary

Australia has a very good superannuation system; in fact it's the envy of the world. It's not perfect, but it has heaps of tax advantages, it's protected by legislation, it's obligatory, it's professionally managed (for those who want it), it has a

TIPS WHEN DEALING WITH A FINANCIAL ADVISER

Most people are in the dark before they go to an adviser. They don't know what to expect or whether they're getting good service. My tips and questions are basic, but they might help:

- Read the financial services guide provided by the planner and ask plenty of questions about their education.
- Ask how long they've been doing this, and what their track record of success has been. Do they have expertise in the thing you most need?
- Ask what services and products they are authorised to provide.
- How do they charge and how much do they charge? Is their fee structure easy to understand?
- If their first manoeuvre is to get you out of the fund you're in and put you in another, do they have evidence that shows this would be best for you? If they don't, why are they doing it? (Remember—it's your money and you can ask any question you want.)
- Always demand alternative strategies. Is it worth your while opening a self-managed super fund? Can your planner give you access to wholesale products which generally work out cheaper? Ask questions and make sure the adviser can explain your investment strategy

in plain English so you understand what's happening to your money.

- Use an adviser who talks about 'discipline', structure and long-term investing. The best-returning funds often just follow the ASX All Ords or the S&P 200 over a decade. An adviser who thinks they can pick winners may be having a lend of you.
- Once you've set the goal and agreed on the strategy, try to stick with it. If you have a large goal, and after adding back you need an annual return of over 10 per cent, you're going to be in volatile territory and you'll have to endure some quarters when you're either going backwards or are well beneath where you wanted to be. The higher the returns the more volatility, and so the longer you have to leave your money in. Advisers tell me that the 'micro-managers'—usually men—do not do as well as the 'little old ladies' who set and forget, and stick with the strategy. Remember: discipline.

large adviser industry behind it, it has choices for every risk and return appetite, and it provides cheap, convenient insurance for those who usually wouldn't have it.

But like all investments, there are basic principles you need to follow:

- **Goal:** Work out how much you're aiming to retire on and then use calculators to see how much you'll have to put in. Be clear about what the goal is, and finetune when necessary.

- **Strategy:** Be clear about how you're going to achieve the goal and what you'll do about the associated risks. Understanding your risk profile, diversification, inflation and market sentiment are crucial starting points.
- **Discipline:** All good investment strategies run on discipline. If you're unsure about when to swap funds or whether to put more money into super or into a mortgage etc., then you have to find and enlist those with the expertise to tell you.

6

YOUR OWN SHARE PORTFOLIO

There's no end to the number of organisations wanting you to place all of your investments into their funds as superannuation. This is their business, and they're very good at getting money into their funds. With a government-mandated private superannuation scheme driving things along, super funds have $1 trillion under management with about $7 billion per quarter flowing into them. Some of them are even very good at investing your money. Most of the time. The Australian superannuation industry is heavily regulated to ensure that the people who manage your retirement money know what they're doing and are honest as well. So—as we've discussed in the previous chapter—superannuation is a good bet, especially when you take into account the tax advantages, the compounding effect and the fact that professionals are keenly focused on inflation risk in a way that hobbyists might not be.

We also know about property. All the calculators for what you need in retirement—all of the economists' assumptions and the actuaries' forecasts—are based on a home with no mortgage. So you need property too, and I advocate that those with the financial capacity also focus on having an investment property by the time they retire.

But the third piece of the retirement savings puzzle should really be establishing and growing your own share portfolio.

Why have a share portfolio?

A personally owned share (otherwise known as equity) portfolio isn't a rejection of the superannuation funds that most Australians use and use successfully. And it's not an either/or choice with your home or investment properties. It's actually a further diversification device for your money; it's a chance to grow your spare money incrementally and separately from your main super and property interests; it has liquidity advantages in that you can access this portfolio whenever you want; and you can access it in increments if you need to, as opposed to having to sell a whole property.

So the benefits are:

- Diversification—away from property, fixed interest and cash
- Liquidity—usually a three-day turnaround
- Dividend income—the average return is around 3.5 per cent

- Growth—long-term capital gains
- Tax effectiveness—through the use of franking credits.

Many Australians believe in bricks and mortar. But for most people who already have the family home, the investment property and super, a further investment in property would be making property an overweighted asset in your personal mix. Let's say you have a $500,000 house, a $300,000 rental apartment and $200,000 in super. You're already overweight on property. If you went out and bought another investment apartment for $300,000, then you'd be very dependent on the property market. You think property is conservative—and historically it is—but on your own balance sheet it will start to look aggressive. You're essentially betting on property. If you can find the deposit to get that new investment apartment, then you can find the $20,000 or $30,000 it takes to kick-start a share portfolio of your own, either via managed funds or direct shares.

I've already discussed the risk elements in super—it's reliant on politicians and legislation. All your assumptions about how much you can make in super and how easily you can use it when you retire are based on what happens in Canberra.

Super is a long-term investment that can't be accessed until you are a certain age. Super calculators rely on all sorts of assumptions about what the market will be doing over a period of time. It's tough to pick the best person to manage your money, so it can be a risk to rely totally on super and put all available cash into it.

Diversification

This whole discussion about property, superannuation and investment is really just about diversification. Let me give you a simple example. If you're working and you have a super fund looking after your retirement savings—whether it's a bank, a life insurance fund or a union fund—you've probably been sent literature from these funds about how tax effective it is to put any bonuses, inheritances or other windfalls into superannuation.You get the tax effective part of it and you get to boost your savings. A lump sum of $10,000 dropped into superannuation when you're 40, assuming you get a return of about 8.5 per cent, is going to be worth more than $75,000 when you're 65. But that same lump sum can also be used on your mortgage: if you have a $300,000, 25-year mortgage and five years into the repayment you put $10,000 straight on top of the mortgage, you save 18 months off the term and more than $30,000 in repayments. If it's the primary home you live in then it's a tax-free improvement to your balance sheet.And remember, once the money goes into super, you may not be able to get it out for a very long time.

These two outlets for spare cash are well understood. But what about your own share portfolio? What about a collection of shares that grows alongside your super and property? Similar calculations can be made for starting a portfolio with the same lump sum.The top 300 companies in the Australian Stock Exchange, known as the ASX 300, have, combined, returned about 13 per cent per annum over the last decade. That's with both share price growth and dividend payouts being reinvested into the market. So if you can get a 13 per cent total return a year, then $10,000 invested wisely at age 40 will be worth more than $200,000 at 65. (This doesn't take into account the tax you have to pay on the dividends you receive, so the final figure depends on the tax bracket you're in.)

When you commit to reinvesting dividends as further share purchases of the same stocks, the compound effect of share investing becomes dramatic, regardless of the taxes you pay. If you want to see how fast a portfolio could grow before you retire, go to Understanding Money (www.understandingmoney.gov.au/content/default.asp) or ASIC's FIDO site at www.fido.asic.gov.au/fido/fido.nsf/byheadline/Calculators?openDocument and have a play with different assumptions. The numbers will speak for themselves.

If this just confuses and scares you, you're not alone. Until 2005, I'd never properly engaged with the share markets. When I was a young accountant doing structured finance for the oil and gas industry, I took an occasional suggestion from a stockbroker mate. In one really bad episode I lost a lot of money—leveraged out of the family home—because I quite simply didn't know what I was doing. I thought it was a game, and that the aim of the game was to get close to the person who had some kind of unique and special insight. Unfortunately those people don't really exist, and if they do, they're insider-trading—a criminal act.

When I realised this in my late twenties, I decided to stay away from direct investment in shares. I was comfortable with property development and building up companies. I knew the risks and returns and I had some luck and some good partners. But having come back to the share investing scene as a more cautious and educated person, and with the insights gained from some of the world's biggest investment banks, I've come to the conclusion that Australians who already have their home organised and their super covered, and perhaps an investment property, should be concentrating on getting a share portfolio started.

Your own portfolio balances the risks of your property, which is usually one asset in one location. It also supports your superannuation savings.

Diversifying timelines

If you remember back to what we said about diversification you'll remember that it's one of the most important asset-protection devices. Most discussions about diversification rightly focus on balancing a portfolio for sector risk, asset-class risk, geographic risk and, in some cases, fund manager risk. When I decided I had to learn something about investing, I certainly followed this last one: I ended up having my money invested with seven different fund managers.

But there's another way of diversifying your assets, and that is diversifying your timelines. Most of the literature you read on diversifying your portfolio is about bonds, shares, property and cash, and having international markets balancing your domestic investments. You also want a spread of industries: what's the point of having your entire portfolio invested in banks and resources companies, or in Sydney property?

But the people telling you all about diversification usually omit the important consideration of the time or the term of your investment. If your retirement is riding on a bunch of assets that mature in your mid-sixties, you're placing all your fortunes in a narrow band of opportunity. Yes, you can take your super as an allocated pension or you can leave the investment earning in your super until you want to drag it all out—maybe it will make more money when the market comes back? But most people have a strategy that's ready for the day they retire. That's when the super has to be cashed in or sold into an annuity structure, or rolled onto the mortgage, etc. This represents timing risk—you could easily be at the mercy of a slumping market or caught in an historic correction of some sort. Perhaps property is in a slump and the assumptions of what you can sell your house for are not going to stack up? Life can be complex and I'm sure every reader can think of a slightly different scenario which would put all of those plans onto the backburner. Not having what you need when you need it is risk; it's actually about volatility, which is how financial markets measure risk.

So I suggest you have a portfolio of shares that you control completely and which you have the choice of how to use. It could be that you sell it when you feel it's peaked, or that you use the portfolio as an income engine in retirement. You may never touch it; it could become a hobby, or something you develop as a fund for the kids' weddings or helping with their first homes. It could be the holiday fund—the savings that fund those cruises or treks.

The point is the choice and flexibility you enjoy with it from a timing perspective: I love property as an investment, but its weakness is that it has to be sold 100 per cent or not at all. Yes, you can rent it out and derive income from it, but it's hard to leverage lump sums out of a property portfolio without selling a property or borrowing against it. And when you're retired, your income is so low that you won't be able to borrow much money. And I've already been through some of the problems with super.

So, I put it to you that you need your own share portfolio, not to compete with property and super but to both augment them and act as a safety net.

So, what do you do and where do you start?

Investment strategy

First, you need to come to an understanding of your strategy. I spoke about this in Chapter 1—the need to understand four Key Concepts (income, risk, diversification and market sentiment) and to use them to synthesise a strategy that works for you. It doesn't matter what you're investing in, these Key Concepts are at the heart of everything. Everyone from the world's largest fund managers to the person with a $5000 share portfolio is using these concepts to manage their assets.

I believe it's also important for these Key Concepts to inform your investment strategy, rather than the other way around. Anyone can go to a get-rich-quick seminar and learn how to leverage their home into more apartments, or how to borrow a ton of money to buy a huge portfolio of shares. Just being handed the strategy is a dangerous shortcut. Whether you use a professional adviser or do some research yourself—and most of this information is available online—I reiterate what I said in Chapter 1: every Australian needs to understand their own retirement strategy. This is why the best fund managers include thumbnail material on these concepts in their pamphlets and ask their customers to use an adviser if they don't understand the concepts. They know that you can talk about concepts, but you can't outsource a strategy: if the investor doesn't understand it—or the key concepts behind it—then it's not really a strategy. It's an accident waiting to happen. I agree. I urge anyone reading this book to go over the Key Concepts—income, risk profile, diversification and market sentiment—and understand how they work before going to the strategy stage.

The second decision brings us into the strategy: Do I want my share portfolio to be a managed fund or do I want to manage it myself with direct shares? Or do I want a mix of both?

This takes us back to the concept of both knowing your own risk profile and understanding the need for diversification. If you can get these two core concepts sorted out to your own satisfaction—without having too many people telling you what to do—then you're already a long way ahead of most Australians.

In the case of the decision about using managed funds or direct shares, the answer is not as clearcut as it may have been ten years ago. Back then, managed funds were largely for conservative investors and direct shares were for those with a greater appetite for risk. But now there are some quite volatile and high-return/high-risk managed funds, which the funds management business calls 'aggressive'. Likewise, there are conservative share portfolios which are heavily weighted in 'defensive' stocks such as insurance and bank shares.

The flipside is that it's much easier for individuals to own shares directly, thanks to the rise of online discount brokers and the sale of one-time government companies such as Telstra.

So it's not as easy as saying that risk averse people should go into managed funds, and those with higher risk profiles should invest directly in shares. In general, the fund managers will have a share fund that matches your risk profile. And if you only want to 'buy the market'—that is, you just want your money to track the All Ordinaries Index—the fund managers have a product for that too at relatively low cost. If you want the risk and diversification worries taken out of your hands, and you're prepared to pay between 1 per cent and 2.5 per cent as a management fee for the privilege, funds might be the best thing for you. But remember you're paying for it. I suggest you have a good look at a site like Money Management, which is a website for financial planners. It includes rankings of all sorts of funds, by Standard & Poor's, and I suggest that you spend some time looking at this sort of material and getting a feel for what's out there. This is an important step. Sometimes too much information is as dangerous as too little, and the managed funds business can be daunting when you first look at it. The Morningstar organisation, for instance, has 49 different fund *categories*, from 'Equity Region Australia Mid/Small Growth' to 'Equity World Large Growth' to 'Multisector: Aggressive' to 'Alternative: Global Hedge Funds', and all possible variations in between.

Managed funds are usually the choice of people who want to simplify their lives and don't want to get bogged down in all the details of investing. But as you see from Morningstar's categories, you still have to select what area of investing you want to be in. And to do that you have to understand your risk appetite, your need for diversification, the market sentiment of various sectors and your goals as they relate to returns via capital growth and income.

But let's first look at the basic pros and cons, comparing managed funds and buying direct shares.

Managed funds versus direct shares

Advantages of managed funds

Managed funds have been popular for many years as an easy way of investing in the stock market and achieving diversification across many stocks. There are several advantages:

- They're easy to access and you can invest small amounts of money very easily.
- You can drip-feed money in direct debits or one-off lump sums, thereby growing an investment incrementally.
- They are a fast track to diversification—some funds are a full diversification strategy in a single fund, covering property, fixed interest, and domestic and global shares in different industry sectors.
- Information and performance data are widely available, and loads of competition means you have choice.
- There is full disclosure of management fees (although they are not always easy to find).
- There is regular reporting.
- You can 'gear' managed funds, thereby creating more potential upside (and downside) with the use of borrowed money.

Disadvantages of managed funds

But managed funds also have their faults, and they are not insignificant:

- You pay management fees and sometimes these are considerable, particularly when the investment is in more exotic assets like international shares. Managed funds also have a wide array of fees that they can levy, and these can be confusing.
- Most of the retail funds pay commissions to the financial planner or adviser who channelled you into the fund. Working out those commissions can be tough work and I'm not convinced that funds paying commissions to advisers is a good idea. It makes me wonder whether the adviser is working for me or for the managed fund.
- The people who run managed funds are judged on their pre-tax performance, but investors are interested in post-tax results—how much they'll end up with in their pockets. That means the fund manager's and the investor's interests are not always aligned. In other words, managed funds can be very tax ineffective.
- Mostly you pay the management fees even if they lose money in a reporting period.
- There can be delays in redemptions of units in managed funds, meaning it takes time to get your money. If you want to get out of your investment, it might take a few weeks.
- Performance reporting lag means that you're always

looking in the rear vision mirror in terms of the real performance of your fund. The 'herd mentality' or the 'lemming effect'—call it what you will, it's a fact that most Australian managed funds invest in the same stocks as one another. In this environment it's hard to have a truly outstanding fund—they follow one another up and they follow one another down.

- Buy-sell spread—not a well-documented part of the funds management business, but do be aware that when you buy into a managed fund you're buying units in a trust. When you invest, you pay a margin over the market unit price to own those units; when you leave the fund, you sacrifice a margin on the sale price of your units. This is the 'buy-sell spread', and the difference goes to the fund manager or stockbroker.

Advantages of direct shares

So how does buying shares directly compare? Some of the advantages are as follows:

- You can buy and sell stocks on a daily traded market, meaning there's plenty of liquidity.
- High amounts of information, regulation and disclosure are available. Media coverage makes it easy to start following high-profile companies or sectors.
- Discount and online brokers make it very cheap to buy shares—about $30 per trade, and much cheaper than it was ten years ago.

- Access to deep information and historical performance data allows for informed decisions.
- There are many layers of the stockbroking industry catering to exactly your level of investment: you can go to a discount-transaction-only broker and pay bottom dollar, or you can have an adviser or a managed portfolio and pay the fees that go with these.
- You can create a portfolio based on higher-yielding, fully-franked company shares, and by the time you retire you can have a whole alternative source of income in addition to your super annuity.
- If your portfolio has only five or six stocks in it, you can shift strategies very quickly and hold your money in cash management accounts until you're ready to invest again.
- You can gear yourself into share portfolios, which increases your risk but also increases your ability to make money—it's called 'leverage'. A margin lending account allows you to borrow money to buy shares, using your established share portfolio as collateral. This is how most investors create leverage in their share portfolios.

Disadvantages of direct shares

Of course investing in direct shares also has its risks:

- Daily traded markets can turn very fast—up or down.
- If you're naturally nervous, you may pull your money at

the worst possible time—when your stocks are sliding and every other amateur is pulling their money out of the same stock.

- Geared portfolios can accelerate your gains on a stock but they can also accelerate your losses; you can end up owing more than you made and being turned off the stock market forever.
- If your strategy is to pick winners, you could be on a losing bet—especially when you consider that you're playing against professionals who do nothing but this.
- You have to track your own trades, capital gains and dividend income; even if you have a 'wrap account' that promises to do the reporting, it's still your responsibility to tell the Tax Office and to ensure the information is correct.

Building your portfolio

Let's get into the actual strategy for a share portfolio. And let's also understand that the strategy you learn here can be used for both direct shares and managed funds.

There are a couple of assumptions we have to start with, and they are that you have the discipline to follow your strategy, and that you see share investing as at least a medium- to long-term activity. When you see the strategy, you'll see why it's important to start thinking like a pro. This style of approach means you can weather disappointments without panicking, knowing that it's the disciplined strategists who win in years five, six and seven, while the panicking amateurs have done their dough and sold out in years one, two and three. Read that last sentence again. Every time I've heard an investment professional lamenting the fortunes of enthusiastic amateurs, this is the bones of what they say: that amateurs lose their money because they can't stick with the strategy they chose; they panic, they flee and they almost always sell when they should hold.

Top 20 Yielders

Here is an investment strategy that actually works: I call it the Top 20 Yielders, and it has been around in many guises for about 80 years.

When I was going from bank to bank and stockbroker to stockbroker, looking for the best strategy for my own retirement needs, the strategy that impressed me most in terms of its longevity of success, its low overheads and its practicality was the one they showed me at Merrill Lynch Private Wealth Services in Sydney. It's not a strategy exclusive to that investment bank, and different institutions add their own bells and whistles. But the following is a simplified version of what Merrill Lynch told me (they use it with their wealthiest clients). I thank Peter Opie—first vice president, investments at Merrill Lynch—for sharing the basics of the strategy with me.

The goal of the Top 20 Yielders strategy is to build a portfolio of stocks that's always producing both capital growth and income. It then relies on the magic of the

BEST OF THE BEST

Two of the greatest stock market investors on Wall Street over the last 120 years are Jesse Livermore and Warren Buffett. And they took polar-opposite approaches to investing. Livermore was known as 'The Great Bear of Wall Street' because he had an uncanny knack for picking the periods of negative returns on Wall Street. He was pure speculator, meaning he traded stocks regularly, punting that he could buy stocks when they were cheap and sell them when they were expensive, thereby beating the market. He traded from the late 1890s till his suicide in 1940. He was one of the few traders to make money, and plenty of it, from the Wall Street crashes of 1907 and 1929.

Buffett has been investing for the last 40 years through his investment and insurance company Berkshire Hathaway. He is a pure 'buy and hold' man: he buys shares and almost never sells.

As you can probably tell by now, my investment philosophy, whether it be property or shares, is more aligned with Buffett. But it's interesting that both Livermore and Buffett held the same view about what stocks to buy. Both believed in holding a small number of stocks, and that those stocks should be market leaders. How can an individual understand 50 different companies? It's a much better idea to concentrate on a few leading companies and get to know them, understand what they do and how they operate—understand their personalities.

In other words, keep your portfolio simple. Look for market leaders in a few different sectors.

It's great advice. How can any person off the street hope to understand dozens of different companies? And if you don't understand them, how will you know which ones to buy and sell?

In other words, keep your share portfolio simple. Hold only a handful of stocks—perhaps a couple of banks, a couple of resource stocks, a retailer and a construction company and maybe a telecommunications company. Read about them and understand them. Also, find a broker or adviser you like and stick with them. Follow these rules and you'll have a much better chance of controlling your portfolio.

compounding effect because both the capital growth and the income from the shares (the dividend yield) are reinvested straight back into the portfolio.

It fulfils via shares what I also insist on for superannuation and property: it produces income and growth. So it fits my goals, my risk profile and my world view.

There are four components to the strategy. The first component is that you select your stocks only from the Top 20 companies on the ASX, by market capitalisation. Merrill Lynch look at the Top 50, but they're professionals.

For amateurs, I think the Top 20 is safer and will ensure you're exposed only to the largest, most stable and liquid companies. These are the only stocks you look at. You must be disciplined about this.

The second component is that you look through your Top 20 stocks and make a list of stocks with a dividend yield that is near, or preferably more than, the cash rate. The cash rate is the official interest rate set by the Reserve Bank of Australia and is the basis for market interest rates. You can find this information in the 'yield' section of the stock charts in the *Australian Financial Review*. You can find the cash rate in the *AFR* too.

The third component is that, on day one, you buy a portfolio of your stocks, the best ones first. If you have only \$5000 or \$10,000, you buy the highest-yielding four or five stocks. You don't worry about sector diversification at this stage—you buy the highest-yielding of the Top 20 stocks.

Over the years you'll build up your portfolio in size and value.

The final component is that you're disciplined enough to revisit these stocks once a year. Each year the strategy remains the same: buy only the stocks that come with a high dividend yield and sell the stocks that no longer meet that requirement. To make sure you get tax advantages of holding stocks for more than a year, you need to turn them over after one year and one day because shares held for more than a year get a capital gains tax concession.

You must be disciplined about this and do what the pros do: stick to the strategy and never 'fall in love' with a stock.

It works like this: let's say I have a windfall from work—a bonus of $5000. My mortgage is looking good and the employer is putting into my super like clockwork. So I decide it's time to get my own portfolio going.

I apply the first component and create my investment 'universe' of the Top 20 stocks on the ASX. I notice that there's a predominance of banks, resource companies, and retailers in my list (note that some people's version of this strategy will exclude property companies).

Next, I go down my list of 20 and strike out the ones with a dividend yield figure substantially less than the cash rate. My universe will not include giving risk capital to companies for almost the same rate that I can have risk-free money in the bank.

This list could come down to eight or nine stocks. So we have a choice to make. And this is why I feel it's important to understand our Key Concepts before getting into strategy. You now have choices about whether you're going to create your Top 20 Yielders portfolio out of bank stocks, resources, retail, media, construction, brewers or financial services stocks. And a certain giant telco called Telstra.

The approach is to ignore what sectors the yielders are from, and buy the highest yielders. With a stock portfolio worth at least $150,000, I believe the natural selection process and size of the portfolio would create a de facto diversification.

But if you have $5000, you would realistically be looking at buying three or maybe four stocks to kick-start your yielders portfolio. And if you're conservative or risk averse you might want to diversify this small selection of stocks. If you have all your money in banks, and banks have a bad year, you're being hit on all sides with no balancing stocks that might be doing better. So what do you do—take a mix of banks and resources and Telstra?

You've already understood your risk profile, the need for diversification, and market sentiment. So you might start off with one each of a bank, a resource company, a retailer and Telstra. You might have other reasons to double up. You might only invest in two of the stocks, or three. It doesn't matter—what matters is that you understand what you're doing, why you're doing it and what the risks and rewards are.

But let's say you invested the $5000 in the highest yielders, and they were a bank, resource company, retailer and Telstra.

You now leave the portfolio for one year and one day.

In 366 days your job is simple: you run the same Top 20 Yielders list, cull the ones that no longer make it, keep the ones that do, and add in the new ones. There's one proviso to this part of the strategy: your job is to look at the stocks that still technically make your list and then have a closer look at the yield figure compared to the share price.

Let's say you bought a $10 stock that was paying a 70c dividend, or 7 per cent. Now, you look at the share price and it's $20, but the dividend is still 70c. The dividend is now actually 3.5 per cent; you fight with your instincts—you see the capital growth reflected in the doubled share price, but—you know what?—you must cull this stock.

Part of your strategy is a return on the risk you are taking. So what to do? Sell it, take the capital gain, and reinvest the profits into your yielders portfolio with a stock that is paying a dividend above the cash rate.

This is an old professional's approach to investing. In the Merrill Lynch case, their Sydney office has been doing this for private clients for 21 years. Since 1985, the All Ordinaries Index has returned an average 11.2 per cent per annum; over the same period the Merrill Lynch yielders strategy has returned 19.8 per cent for clients.

Yes, it is conservative but it works over the long haul, which is really the only way most investors make money from shares. Successful investors also have discipline.

The goal of this strategy is to build a portfolio of thirteen stocks, and build it over time so that by the time you're in retirement you've amassed a portfolio—in a relatively risk-friendly way—that has at its heart the historical capital growth performance of Top 20 ASX stocks, and the income flows of the higher-yielding companies. These two factors together create that powerful compounding effect, especially if you're prepared to plough the dividends straight back into your portfolio, and also if you're prepared to sell the growth stocks that have fallen behind on dividend yield. That's where the profits come from—culling out the capital growth and recycling back into the portfolio.

There are a few concepts in this strategy that perhaps I should elaborate on. The first is the question of how the dividend yield of a stock refers to the share price. This is a crucial issue because this is how the portfolio makes such good gains with relatively low risk. Dividend yield is always calculated as a percentage of the value of the company—its market capitalisation. So when there's a high-yielding stock it may mean the market has undervalued the stock. In that case, high yield equals low share price.

You hold such a stock for one year and one day and on average you'll be getting that stock at the start of an upswing in share price. This is the attraction of buying Top 20 stocks—they will almost always come back to the pack in share price because they are highly traded, large brand-names that will eventually be bought again by the big institutional investors. So, in simple terms, you buy high yield/low price for the certainty of return, and when the price goes up and the yield goes down to a lower percentage, you sell, take the capital growth and reinvest in a high yielder again. Twelve months seems to be the optimum frequency for doing this.

Choosing from the Top 20 means stability and long-term performance indicators on well-known stocks, and you're always giving yourself a chance of making both income and capital growth because your strategy is always one or the other. As long as you're disciplined and can stick to the strategy, you'll make stable returns.

Being a somewhat conservative person myself, you can see why I'm most comfortable with my money being managed in this manner: buying stocks on yield makes me relax because I know that I start from an advanced position where I'm guaranteed of making money. As I write this, all of my yielder stocks are earning dividend yields in the 6 to 7 per cent range. Then there's share price appreciation on top, which in recent years has been considerable. When you consider that the average total return on 'balanced' managed funds is 8.5 per cent you can see why I like the Top Yielders approach.

Remember this also: in the last 20 years the All Ordinaries Index has performed at a rate of 11 per cent per annum compound; and 6 per cent of that has been from income.

I also like the fact that there's a protection device inbuilt: because you're only buying stocks from the top of the pile, when the market goes down—and it will always go down at some point—there's generally a flight to quality shares. And when that happens the shares you've invested in may actually go up. You take the capital growth and reinvest in the high yielders again, which as we know are the low share prices. You are always riding a market cycle rather than trying to pick winners. And when you're doing that, you're tuning in to market sentiment rather than trying to outsmart everybody else.

The other part of this strategy I like is that you annually 'turn over' the portfolio, but you don't 'sell' it. You instead reinvest all dividends and capital growth and allow the miracle of compounding to work its magic. Compounding is best illustrated by the 'Rule of 72'. (Mathematically, if you're being paid an interest rate of 7.2 per cent per annum, your money will double every ten years.) So, if you start a yielder portfolio with $20,000 and it averages

7.2 per cent, that's $40,000 in ten years. If the portfolio makes 14 per cent per annum (not out of the question), you double your money in six years. In 20 years it's worth $275,000.

A $50,000 yielders portfolio will be worth $687,000 in 20 years if it averages 14 per cent per annum. That's without borrowing more money to accelerate it, which is what many people do. And all you did was follow a simple, conservative strategy that can be run from the kitchen table and involves only an hour of your time each year and one phone call to a broker.

Over time the portfolio will grow, and you may think you need more diversity because you don't want a big lump of money concentrated in a few stocks in Australia. Your Top 20 Yielders strategy could become the Top 50 Yielders strategy, or you could expand into US and UK markets. But, as always, understand the strategy and know how your Key Concepts operate in offshore markets.

Investing in managed funds

The other way to get your own portfolio happening is via managed funds. There are hundreds of managed fund products in Australia, and most of them are retail funds that allow anyone to invest with amounts as low as $1000.

Within the plethora of choices, there are two basic styles of investing in shares via managed funds: you either 'buy the market' or you buy a fund that tries to 'outperform the market'.

What does this mean? It simply means that you're placing your money either with a manager who promises to return at least the performance of a certain market index—usually the All Ordinaries Index or the S&P/ASX 200—or you're putting your money with a manager who tries to pick winners, with an aim to outperform those major indices.

There's something else to remember with funds: you can invest in them directly via online organisations such as CommSec and Direct Access and get the forgone financial planner's fee rebated to you. Doing it this way boosts your investment right from the start, but you still need to know what you're doing and why you're doing it. I can't tell you what your risk profile is or what returns you need to generate. What I can say is that, if you use a fund to invest in equities, you have a clear ability to judge the performance of these managers. All share markets have an index which measures how well the market performed in a given year. In Australia we have the All Ordinaries Index and the S&P/ASX 200, in the US it's called the Dow Jones Industrial Average or the S&P 500, in London it's the FTSE, and in Hong Kong it's the Hang Seng. The best known measure of global share indices is called the MSCI. Your job is to know what these benchmarks are, and whether the funds you're looking at—or are invested in—are matching or outperforming the market. And you need to remember that the managed funds figures you're looking at don't include the effects of tax or any 'advice' fees. And the extra costs can be substantial.

With indices, they go back in historical series and you can find them online. Simply look back over, say, five years, see what the S&P/ASX 200 was doing each year, then compare that with the historical performance of the fund you're looking at. This is one of the big advantages of fund managers—their levels of disclosure and performance data are very good, and with so much information there's no excuse for you not to observe basic due diligence.

The Top 20 Yielders strategy is simple and effective for buying shares, and you can do similar things with managed funds: set yourself a timeframe of a year, and always balance your portfolio of managed funds in terms of which ones are in, say, the second quartile of performance. As already noted, the problem with chasing the top quartile performers is that their brief moment in the sun is often followed by a swift fall back into the pack. In the managed funds world—especially the 'balanced' and 'income' funds—outperforming the mob is a correction waiting to happen. But the second quartile powers along without the ups and downs. You can also spread yourself more easily with managed funds since there are ones that are global, ones that target industries, sectors and even other funds, and ones that simply track indices.

Borrowing to invest

Talking about building your own portfolio leads to the question of geared investing—borrowing money to buy shares.

TAX ON SHARES

Too many investors don't think about the tax they have to pay on capital gains when they trade in the stock market. It needs to be part of every investment decision, particularly since investments in super, and property in which you live, pay a much lower rate of tax. If you've held a share for a few years and then the price drops sharply, or you think it might drop sharply, you might be tempted to sell out. But in all likelihood you'll have a capital gain on those shares, and that's money you must have available to pay the Tax Office. The end result might not be as good as you'd hoped.

Let's take the example of an investor who purchased $10,000 worth of shares in a company four years ago. Let's say those shares are now worth $13,000. Suddenly that stock's price drops 10 per cent. The shares are now worth $11,700. The investor decides to sell out. They have to pay capital gains tax on the $1700 capital gain they've made. They've held the shares for more than twelve months, and assuming their marginal tax rate including the Medicare levy is 46.5 per cent, then after tax the shares are worth a little over $11,300. That means the investor put in $10,000 and four years on has made only $1300 after tax.

There are a few distinct ways to do it and they all have their supporters. But however you gear an investment, there's one thing worth remembering: while borrowing more can amplify your gains, it can also multiply your losses. I strongly urge anyone who's been approached to do this kind of investing to get independent advice before going ahead. Have a chat with an accountant or a knowledgeable financial planner you trust and get to the bottom of this style of investing.

The simple illustration is to turn the advertising on its head: yes, a 5 per cent upward movement in a share price might get you a $1000 gain, or $3000 if you're geared. But the converse works too: you can lose $1000 if the share price slides 5 per cent, and you lose $3000 if you're geared into the same share. Plus, when you borrow to invest, you have interest rates which charge against your account regardless of what the share price is doing.

I've talked about inflation risk in this book, and will keep talking about it. Just because you're buying shares, and just because you're borrowing to do so, doesn't mean that inflation doesn't apply to you. It does, and it's your job to know what you're making or losing year on year. If you're not beating 3 per cent, you're not beating inflation. Money in shares is risk money invested in a business. It must reward the fact that you're assuming risk.

Also, when you gear you have borrowing costs. Whatever you think you're earning, you must offset it against the price of the debt, and the fact that the lenders take your house as security. Always be aware of what you're doing on all fronts.

There are no free lunches in the markets.

Margin lending

The most common geared way into the stock market is margin lending. You do this through a stockbroker or a bank; they make money available on an ongoing basis from which you can 'draw down' credit to buy shares. It's like an investor's overdraft. The lender insists on lending ratio limits—usually 75 per cent geared is the limit. That means that if you're buying $10,000 worth of shares, you must have at least $2500 of your own money to put towards the purchase. If the value of a portfolio goes down sufficiently to put you over your limit (that is, the debt component of your margin lending portfolio goes beyond 75 per cent), the lender makes a 'call', which means you have to come up with enough money to reduce your gearing back to your limit. Using the $10,000 example, if the shares dropped in value to $9500 and you'd borrowed $7500 your gearing ratio would now be 79 per cent, above the limit. In this example you would have to come up with an extra $375 to pay to the lender to get the gearing level back to 75 per cent.

Margin lending is booming. As of 2006 it had increased five-fold in seven years to be worth $25 billion in outstanding loans. Average gearing levels for portfolios are still around 42–45 per cent, which is historically low, and low by world standards. But the Reserve Bank of Australia has warned about single-stock margin lending portfolios—when you borrow to buy one stock. The RBA says more than one-third of margin loans in 2006 were single-stock portfolios. I have nothing against gearing to increase your upside, so long as you know what you're doing or you're being advised by someone who does. But a single-stock portfolio? Forget it—it sounds either lazy or speculative. Have a think about whether that type of thing fits with your risk profile or your diversification strategy.

There *is* a bonus with margin lending: margin loan debt is tax deductible in the same way as the interest on an investment property loan is tax deductible. And the assessable capital gains is discounted by 50 per cent if the investment is held for more than one year.

Secured loans

You don't have to go into a draw-down facility in order to gear a share investment. Some people simply borrow, say, $100,000 against their house and invest it in a portfolio of shares. You don't have to worry about the value of this going up and down and triggering a margin call; you can set it and forget it—in the same way as for the Top 20 Yielders—and have a plan where the loan is paid out by the returns; or you can take an interest-only loan and sell the portfolio in ten years' time, and you keep the difference between the initial loan and the sale price of your portfolio. Many planners do it this way so they can structure the deal to suit the client's circumstances and timelines. The margin lending system is not so flexible.

Investment advisers

If you want to follow the scenario outlined above—the Top 20 Yielders—you may not need much in the way of advice from the financial community. You may be satisfied that you can do it yourself, and that's up to you. But a person's financial affairs are often much more complex than investing in a high-yielding portfolio.

Investors should be aware that stockbroking and financial advice come at a cost. The more you transact with a firm, and the more you rely on the firm for tax, insurance, estate planning and other advice, the more you'll have to pay. For this reason I'm reluctant to nominate what you should be paying and what you should be getting for your money. But at the very least you should find out what services are available and what they cost. And you must make sure that your adviser can explain things to you in terms you understand. At my financial services group, Yellow Brick Road, we pride ourselves on doing this.

Making lasting gains

I suppose the conclusion of this chapter is that there is a proven method used by the professionals to make lasting gains in a share portfolio. But it takes patience, discipline and commitment over time. There are more complex ways of owning a share portfolio, but you'll pay for these and they may represent more time and hassle than you're prepared to devote.

If you don't want to build a portfolio the patient way—starting small with compounding returns and yields—then you have to borrow. The thing to remember with geared shares is that you have an increased cost of ownership: interest. As a person who's been in the property development game for a long time, I've seen a lot of schemes hatched on the back of large debt. I suggest that anyone who wants to borrow a single cent to make money on shares should first sit down and assess the exact costs of borrowing the money and the likelihood that they'll be able to pay back the loan in the time promised. These are the basics of borrowing; it's not like borrowing to buy a house that your family lives in. Investment debt must purchase assets that will yield a high return. You need to think about the debt with reference to a timeframe and a goal for its return. And it won't get you your return if the debt costs too much—tax break or no tax break.

7

THE UNSEXY STUFF

We can try all we like to make the subject of saving for retirement sound interesting and fun, in part so that in years to come our kids will see it as something worth doing and something worth starting early. But there's a whole layer of this which is not really that inspiring for any of us.

I call it the unsexy stuff. It's all those bits and pieces that you know—as an adult—you should be doing, yet you procrastinate. These unsexy things are not the magic of compounding or the inspiration of having your own income stream in retirement. They don't look empowering, they won't directly get you on a cruise ship for that holiday of a lifetime, and they're not the kind of things you boast about at a party.

But they are the things that can stop you going broke, ease the misery for family and business partners, and help people put their lives back on track.

If most of this book has been about building assets and enhancing the yield, then this chapter is about protecting your assets. If you're going to have a really happy retirement, during which you have money and your health, these are the things that have to be done first.

Estate planning

No-one wants to think about what's going to happen when they pass away. But here's a wake-up call: just because it's unpalatable to you, that won't make it any easier for your family to sort out the mess once you've gone and left nothing but confusion and litigation.

As far as I'm concerned, if you're an adult you should have a will. And those with kids should have an enduring power of attorney.

Will

As you build wealth, the assets you develop start to have an impact not just on you but on the people around you. If you have kids, your property and the proceeds of your life insurance policies are massively important for their well-being should you pass away. If you're married, assets such as share portfolios or a business have as much bearing on your spouse when you die as they had on you when you were alive. They are important—they don't just cease to be so because you're not there to enjoy them.

I urge anyone who owns property or shares, who has a life insurance policy or who has kids or a business partner, to go to their solicitor and have a will drawn up. They might ask how you want the funeral to be—burial or cremation—and at which church or other place of worship you want to be remembered in. They'll ask you to assign your property. For people who are married this won't count so much, because joint tenancy title deeds automatically revert 100 per cent of the matrimonial property to the surviving spouse. If you're the surviving spouse, you have to assign the property to those you wish to receive it in your will. By the time you're in retirement, the beneficiaries of your will could include grandchildren, children, staff and business partners. There could be a whole cast of people. And if you've been married a couple of times and have children from those marriages, you have to get really serious.

So it's imperative that you have a solicitor do this right the first time. There's lots of advertising around about making your own will from a will kit; there's also advertising about the dangers of people challenging wills. The best thing you can do is make sure you have the conversation with the solicitor and let them run through the issues. You'll feel much better when you've done this, believe me.

The second point is that you must communicate the intentions of your will to those who benefit. I don't understand the secrecy around this: if you have a will, and you're getting on in years, gather the folks around and have a conversation. When people know where they stand they can clear the air and have the arguments while you're still alive. And there's much less chance of the will being challenged when you're gone.

Enduring power of attorney

An enduring power of attorney is a legal document which assigns the right to a trusted person to step into your legal shoes and act as your proxy should you ever become incapacitated. An enduring power of attorney will be very valuable to your family (and your business if you have one) should you be in that state which is not death, and therefore is not covered by your will or life insurance, yet which sees you incapacitated. Such instances include coma, being kept alive on life support, insanity and senile dementia.

There are plenty of other instances where an enduring power of attorney is useful. The medical and legal fraternities have a long list of the conditions and their severity which are defined as an incapacity. In the end it's usually the doctors and lawyers who make the call. The point is, if you find yourself in this limbo—with all these assets, with bills to pay, school fees, a mortgage—yet no will to execute, you are in a strange legal situation. Your loved ones may find it impossible to get any money released until the state appoints a person to act as your guardian. They are often slow and overworked, and they charge your family many thousands of dollars to administer your affairs while you're incapacitated. It can be a terrible time for the family: not only is there the medical trauma that's happening to you, but life can't go on because simple authorities and pieces of paper can't be signed. Payments get missed.

A simple enduring power of attorney quickly resolves any authority issues and leaves one or two persons clearly in control and with the legal power to go into bank accounts, sell property, pay wages and sign contracts. Depending on which state it is drawn in, it may be a document with clear instructions about vegetative states and whether the machine at some point gets turned off.

Sorry—I told you this was the unsexy stuff. Some of the volatile situations that families get themselves into over this issue of permanent incapacity are terrible to watch. If you have an enduring power of attorney, you not only have a good chance that your assets are being put to good use, but you make it so much easier on the people who have to go on.

By the way, you must tell/ask the person you are appointing, and you may make provision in your finances to pay them for their work. Your solicitor will tell you all about this.

Succession

If you're a business owner, part of your general estate planning should involve the identification and grooming of a successor, and a clear narrative about what happens to the shares or equity you have in the business and who gets to step up or buy in. In many privately owned companies, the founder-owner doesn't want their son or daughter to inherit the equity—they want a talented manager to buy in and keep the firm running. But if something happens to you, how is anyone going to know this if you never wrote it down and made your intentions clear?

If you value the business you built up for years—and the employees who work in it and the family who stand to inherit it—you'll make these simple arrangements as a part of estate planning. Solicitors deal with this every day—they know what to do, and will make suggestions.

Insurance

I've never understood the irritation caused by insurance. It's a product you buy that 'de-risks' the parts of your life that you value. It's that simple. Building retirement assets that create income when you're not working takes time and effort. So they are valuable. You must keep all your assets—including your health and income-earning capacity—covered for the risk that they could be drastically reduced by some of the things that happen in life.

I use an insurance broker because I like to have all my insurance in one place and I like to know I'm getting the best products for the best price. I suggest anyone with more than three or four forms of insurance find a broker and talk about what they need. Brokers keep you covered as your assets grow and don't let inflation erode your cover. They know where the best deals are, which insurers to deal with and which to stay away from. They're experts who will argue your case if need be.

These are the forms of insurance I suggest you buy as you plan for retirement.

Life insurance

Definitely not sexy, but crucial. If you have a mortgage or other liabilities, you need life insurance. Whether you leave kids, a spouse and kids, or a business partner behind, the surviving people will need to be able to pay off debt. That's what life insurance is for. If you doubt you need this, ask yourself one question: could my spouse/partner/children cover the mortgage and credit card payments and car lease and personal loan repayments on their own if I died tomorrow?

If the answer is 'no', you need life insurance.

Income protection

I've said it throughout this book: your ability to create income is your greatest asset. So why wouldn't you insure that asset? If I gave you a $10 million building, the first thing you'd do would be to insure it. It has value. But for some reason the fact that someone can earn $3 million in their working life doesn't seem to have the same impact on them. I say it is the most important thing you have, and if you are injured or ill, you must be able to cover basic expenses that your wages would normally have covered.

Insurers usually don't insure for more than 75 per cent of your salary and you have to elect a waiting period—a length of time that you are incapacitated but don't claim. It can be two weeks, a month or two months. The longer the stand-down period, the lower your premiums. I think this is a great product, especially for anyone who has both kids and a mortgage. One tip: upgrade your policy when you get a pay-rise. Another tip: tradespeople can have a hard time getting this insurance at a price that makes it useful. These people should either get a broker or check with their professional trade association for good income-protection policies or see if there is one available through their super.

House and contents

Stands to reason, doesn't it, that if your whole retirement strategy hinges on having debt-free property, you'd have this central asset insured? Actually, you'd be amazed. Everyone who gets a mortgage in this country has to produce a cover note from an Australian insurance company which shows that the house itself is insured. But it's what happens after that which amazes me. People let their insurance run down, because they can't be bothered changing it or because they don't want to lift the value of the cover and pay the extra premiums. This is another reason for having a broker. They will reset this every year. You'd be surprised what you amass in your house over the years, and how much it's worth. Also, the value of your property goes up, beyond the inflation-based increases your insurer considers: there's capital growth, there's the rise in building costs, there are the capital improvements you have made. The whole point of house and contents insurance is to *replace* what is destroyed or damaged or stolen. If you don't have sufficient cover, you've been wasting your money.

TPD insurance

Total and permanent disability (TPD) insurance is a product that provides you with an agreed payout for events that are not death, but nevertheless incapacitate you to such a degree that you're unlikely to work again. There's a whole schedule of traumas, illnesses and injuries that will trigger payments. I suggest that for this policy you use a broker who knows what to look for and knows the best products. TPD is a very good product and everyone who works and has dependants, and overheads like a mortgage, needs this insurance. However, I would urge you to use a professional to advise and negotiate it for you—TPD is complex.

Private health insurance

If you value your health and wellbeing and the health of your family, this is a great product. In particular, it's going to be something you want in later years when some of your medical ailments might be more serious than they are now. As the population ages, hospital and medical costs are, most likely, going to rise and you'll need to be covered by insurance to access the technology. In terms of my belief that you can plan for good health and vitality in the same way that you can plan your finances, private medical cover is good for all the non-trauma finetuning we do along the way. Most of the funds have cover for wellbeing, alternative healing and fitness programs. A fund like this can actually help motivate you to do more for yourself, and to follow your own health plan.

Funeral bonds

Estates can take a while to clear, and that can leave the loved ones a bit short on money to fund a funeral for you. Funeral bonds allow you to buy now the value of funeral you want in the future and have your investment earning money too. When you die, the bonds are redeemed and the money is used to pay for the funeral expenses. And it should be a lot more than you put in, given that the bonds are investments in fixed interest, cash and mortgages. This is about as unsexy as it gets, but it means protecting what you hold dear, as your immediate family may not have the money to see you off.

Some tips

There are many more forms of insurance you can buy. These are just the basics. My big tip is to use an insurance broker—they're easy to find. My second point is to rethink your reluctance about these products. Think about it as de-risking your life and protecting your assets and the yield they create. Third, life insurance and income protection can often be sourced via your superannuation fund. This was inserted by the union movement in the early 90s as a way to give ordinary working people access to these crucial types of cover. They are tax effective and therefore cheap. But always check with a broker first: they may be able to get you a better product at a better price.

Title deeds

There are a growing number of unmarried property owners who buy their property with another person. They are friends, they are siblings, they are gay couples. They come from all walks of life, and they have one thing in common—they buy their property under a title deed called tenants-in-common.

The tenants-in-common title deed is a legal document that states who owns the property. With a tenants-in-common title, each of the owners owns a portion of the property as equity. They can sell this equity and they can trade it. They own it separately from the other owner.

This is distinct from the joint tenants title, which is generally used by married couples. The joint tenants title means there is in effect a single owner, but there are two people within this single owner entity. If one of the owners dies, all of the title is now in the name of the surviving owner. Neither can own 50 per cent equity and so they can't sell the equity or assign it. What can happen is that one of the parties can force a sale on the other; if one wants to sell, they both have to.

In short, the law has a lot of inbuilt protections for people on a joint tenants title, but there are not as many protections for tenants-in-common. Tenants-in-common have to have a contract.

Before you go into a joint purchase, you should invest in some time with a solicitor who can explain the issues associated with these ownership situations and what happens when they're over. You'll need two things: a contract and a good understanding of the tenants-in-common title. Your agreement must cover who owns what, who's paying what, how the mortgage is to be paid, and an agreement on buy-outs. For instance, if one of the co-owners wants to move on, the other owner should have first right of refusal. But how do you value the share that's for sale? How do you stop people you don't know or don't like becoming co-owners with you? What happens if one of the shareholders dies and doesn't have a will?

No-one likes to think about the day when things may not be so friendly, so get a professional to talk you through it. Property is part of your retirement assets—make sure you protect what's yours.

Divorce

One in three marriages ends in divorce, so let's be grown-ups about this. Just because you have come to the end of the road romantically, it doesn't mean that either party has to suffer financially or in terms of their long-term retirement goals. I urge anyone going through this or leading up to it to hold out for a peaceful solution to the break-up so both parties can enjoy a settlement that keeps some wealth intact. This is especially the case for couples with a business: Who gets the shares? Who values those shares? Often, the husband keeps the company and the wife gets the house.

What if there are two properties? What if there's no property but a big lump of super in the man's name? Women in particular need good legal advice around divorce, and I would urge you to find a lawyer who's devoted to keeping your wealth intact for the future rather than trying to score some sort of 'victory' in court. Good lawyers know how to do this and know how to keep the old arguments out of the new settlement.

Women often put their earning years on hold to have the kids and create a home, so they don't have super. There are plenty of cases where women can get some of the man's super as part of the settlement. I don't think this is harsh—as long as the divorcing wife is rolling her share of the super into her own super, I think it's a good wealth-building idea.

As always, get professional advice on this. Ask around and find a solicitor who's committed to finding a non-rancorous settlement. There's no reason why both divorcing parties can't be financially secure in the future.

Tax

When talking about protecting wealth, many people overlook the obvious: the tax man. Of all the things that can threaten the accumulation of your income-generating assets, taxation is actually the most regular and most certain of the lot. It's the law, there's a large bureaucracy devoted to collecting it from you, and there are large financial penalties for not paying it.

If you pay too much, you lose your yield. If you pay too little, you're fined, and you lose your yield.

Again, under the heading of unsexy, you have to pay for the experts to keep you on the straight and narrow when it comes to tax. It's important, it's complex and it's the kind of thing that experts do best. You need good accountants or lawyers for expert tax advice. It's as simple as that. These are the people who can create for you the right legal and financial structure (trust, company, etc.), advise on the right timing of purchases and sales, and put you in a position where you don't pay too much or too little.

Remember that the assumptions about returns that you base your entire retirement strategy upon are measured in increments of 1 and 2 per cent. Over 20 years, these add up to a lot of money. We've already covered the inflation problem and the shrinking value of your dollar as time goes by, such that a 10 per cent per annum return over ten years is really only 7 per cent. If you make some bad decisions on how you structure your share portfolio, whose name you put your investment property into, or your timing of buying and selling assets, then your 7 per cent is shrinking again.

I mean no offence but financial advisers, accountants and solicitors are not sexy occupations. But experts in those areas will help you protect the assets you own and the yields that come from them. When, at the beginning of this book, I spoke about using experts to help execute the strategy, this is what I was talking about.

If nothing else, having expert advice on things like financial planning and tax gives you peace of mind. And having that when you're retired is something you can't put a price on.

8

THE ULTIMATE INVESTMENT: YOU AND YOUR CHILDREN

The real measure of your wealth is how much you'd be worth if you lost all your money.

Anonymous

It has been striking me lately how strangely focused my generation has become. People born in the 1950s—the baby boomers—are currently obsessed with their retirement savings and making sure they have enough to finance the way they want to live when their incomes stop. It's a good goal, and one we've basically been pushed into by successive governments.

But when I look around at how some of us are travelling in the mental and physical sense, I'm not comforted by what I see. For all this financial discipline and all the plans and the borrowing and the advisers, there are going to be a lot of boomers retiring with a big pile of assets and cash, yet with bodies and minds—and maybe spirits too—that are not going to allow them to enjoy their retirement years.

They're getting the first three right—property, super and shares—but they've missed the most important one of all. Their health and wellbeing: the ultimate investment.

I don't think good health and happiness are accidents. I think we're all born with different strengths, but the vast majority of us can manage our wellbeing with goals, strategies and discipline. The statistics agree: in the United States, going into middle age brings with it heart disease and cancer—these are the diseases that kill people in their sixties and seventies. But here's another fact: if you make it to 75, there's a high chance you'll reach 86. If you live to 80, on average you can expect to live another eight years. In other words, health can be managed, and longevity can be planned in relation to getting past the risks of even just two diseases.

In the Report of the NSW Chief Health Officer (2006) the finding was that 67 per cent of all premature deaths in New South Wales could have been avoided or slowed by improved *management* of individuals' health, including early detection and healthier lifestyles.

In other words, some of your health and wellbeing is a management issue—you can do something about it. The system I've reiterated in this book as it concerns property, super and shares is that you set a goal, develop a strategy and have discipline. This is also how I approach my physical and mental wellbeing. Happiness is a skill, mental acuity is a habit, and fitness is a result of self-management and discipline. How many fit and healthy people in their forties don't work at it? Not many.

When I think about it, I realise my financial goals and success are actually part of a broader scheme for health and happiness. My wellbeing probably sits at the core of who I am, and the money revolves around that core. It's not the other way around.

I believe that investing in your future means investing in yourself. And that means having the mental, physical and spiritual capacity to live life to the fullest during those very years when you're supposed to be doing so.

Good health and happiness

I am 51 years old. I am the chairman of Australian Financial Investments Group (AFIG), a company that owns Wizard Home Loans and other mortgage funding and management entities that handle all the backroom stuff for a lot of mortgage lenders. We have more than 300 branches in Australia and New Zealand, and as I write this we're moving the Wizard branch model into India and other countries—I'm heading up that too, and so I've spent the last two years travelling much more than I would wish. I'm also chairman of Yellow Brick Road Group, a financial services group that offers financial planning and accounting advice, stockbroking, insurance and investing advice. I still own my property development businesses, State Capital Group, I'm on the Eastern Suburbs Rugby League Club board, I have four sons—three of them still teenagers—and I'm an Adjunct Professor of banking and finance at the University of New South Wales. I'm on the board of the Powerhouse Museum and Sport Knowledge Australia, and I'm campaign chairman of The Centre for Children with Cancer. Now I've written it all down I realise I do have a bit on my plate.

I need to take my own counsel. Things creep up on me, and like many people I tend to say yes to more than I should. It's important that every now and then I get into context what I actually do. Just like everyone should.

When I was younger, having this kind of flat-out life seemed normal. I had loads of energy and time, and a lot of my peers were also working too hard. It was what you did. But these days, having turned 50, I'm a prime target for people asking me how I manage it all.

Actually, that's the answer in itself. I manage lots of things: business, people, consulting experts, shareholders, businesspeople. I manage my time, I manage my expectations and I manage disappointment.

It's stressful and tiring. I recently attempted to make myself cut back from the six-day weeks I've been working for 30 years. I've been partially successful in this pull-back, sometimes for long periods. But when I travel I come back to six-day weeks until I've cleared the backlog.

Many people live like this, not just me.

Years ago, when I was still doing structured finance for clients at a law firm, I realised I'd have to also manage my body, mind and spirit or there wouldn't be much left of me at the end of each week to enjoy what my efforts produced.

So, at an age when many of my hard-charging peers in

Sydney's Martin Place finance district were dealing with stress by hitting the booze or quitting the professional life to do something quieter, I embarked on a piece-by-piece system of managing those things that were really at the core of it all. I needed a fit body, I needed a sharp mind and I needed a light spirit. They add up to happiness, I believe.

I wasn't a natural at taking control of these personal issues. I had to think it through, decide what I was going to do, and find ways to make it happen. I started with the issue of how I was going to keep striving without my body giving out, my mind going haywire and my soul getting heavy. That's what I could see happening to people who were ten or fifteen years older than me. From there I got straight to the old techniques that I learned from my mum and dad and that I apply to everything I do: goal, strategy, discipline. I didn't know how to manage my wellbeing, or even how to find the people who could show me, so I went back to what worked in other pursuits.

Goal, strategy, discipline

Everyone who is successful has a goal. It's what they do all the time. It's what makes them succeed. Yet how many people reading this have a goal for their wellbeing? I don't mean looking at a model in a magazine ad and saying 'I'd like to look like that'. I mean a goal like 'I will be able to run 3 km in 20 minutes' or 'I will complete a higher learning course' or 'I will spend at least two hours every week with my kids without taking my mobile phone with me'.

I think many people avoid setting personal goals of the type we're talking about not because they don't want the outcome but because either the strategy is not immediately clear to them and they can't be bothered finding the information, or they know they don't have the discipline and don't want to let themselves down.

Goals are easy. Strategy requires that you go out of your way. Discipline is hard.

Some people get to the strategy stage: they join the gym, they get an evaluation from a professional, they get a tailored exercise program, and the trainer even keeps an eye on them for their first couple of visits. Then what? Three weeks later they stop turning up. They had to work late, they were travelling, they were tired. We all know the excuses, because we all use them from time to time.

The point here is that goals and strategy—while crucial—are never going to work for those who can't follow through with discipline.

If there was money in it, such as a job, these same people would be there and participating with bells on. They don't mind being disciplined by someone else's requirements as to when and how they turn up. But if you tell them that they're investing in themselves, they have every excuse in the book.

This also seems to go for bad diets, smoking and stress. You can show people the goal and you can plot out the strategies. But, left to their own devices, the stressed-out person who has been warned about blood pressure will still bring work home and do things like take the kids to the movies with the mobile phone switched on. We all know people—often men—who've had the official dire warning: that a cocktail of overwork, bad diet and smoking is going to lead to heart disease, stroke, diabetes or any number of stress-related ailments. Yet they can't switch it around and invest something in themselves.

The worst cases I've seen are when a person can't even see the reason for setting goals for better health in the first place. At least the person who tried and then gave up will have a chance of coming back. Me? When I realised that this was all something that could at least be improved by being managed, I started with simple things. My initial personal goals centred on running and the gym. I wanted to be strong and have good cardio capacity, so I exercised six days a week.

Previously I hadn't been exercising enough and I'd been eating bad food. Often I was feeling tired in the middle of the afternoon. I wanted more energy. So I started eating a piece of fruit every day and tried to eat more salads. I cut down on my red meat intake. I started eating nuts between meals, which was good for keeping up my energy levels.

I also set myself the goal of being able to spend proper time with my family and to sleep without my mind interrupting me with stress and worries. So I developed stress-management habits that have stayed with me to this day.

My spirit? I wanted to be happy more often than unhappy—that was the goal. I had read somewhere that ambitious people often forget their happiness because they're always producing rather than receiving. I planned to give back to myself and take a short break once a year where I would travel somewhere that caught my fancy and do nothing but hang around. On my own.

These were pretty rudimentary goals and strategies to put in place on the eve of turning 30. But as I matured I also started taking on the professional advice of doctors and trainers. My early habits didn't really change, but I decided that along with the cardio and strength fitness I should also have flexibility. My goal shifted to being able to retire and still be able to tie my shoes. So, on the advice of some mates in the game, I shifted some of my running and gym time to yoga and stretching. Making a habit of that means

CHOOSE YOUR DOCTOR

Along the way I've come to a conclusion about health professionals: just as there are good and bad financial advisers, there are also good and not-so-good doctors. I personally feel that if you're going to get yourself into shape for your retirement years you're going to have to find a doctor (a physician really) who takes what I call a whole-of-life approach. After all, your health is a whole-of-life issue. You have a mind, you have a body and you have a spirit. And all of them, surely, have to be healthy before you can claim to be in 'good health'?

I should be able to beat the stiff back and locked-up groin that so many men develop in their fifties.

My diet matured too: I now eat less red meat and mostly I consume 'whole food'. I still drink and sometimes I have one beer too many, but mostly I don't. My attitude to stress-relief has also changed over the years. And I've also come to openly think in terms of the soul.

I put it to all readers that these are the kinds of issues they have to work through in their own minds before embarking on a program of good health for the long term.

So here the emphasis is on finding the right health adviser. And that will probably start with a doctor. The kind of advice and management I'm talking about is covered by Medicare as 'health promotion'. There's no excuse not to do it. No excuse not to start investing in yourself. Personally, I go for a check-up and a chat once a year. I have a hundred excuses not to do it, but I do it. I simply don't accept that I don't have the time for my own health. It's my investment in myself.

If you want to know what the professionals think about this, you should hear Professor Ron Penny. His company, Good Health Solutions, advises many large corporations on their staff wellbeing policies and the active management of issues such as diet, exercise, stress and mental health. Ron tells me that not only is health a management issue for people, it's one that has to be planned and worked on: 'Like any good investment, an investment in your health benefits from putting time into it. There's no point getting to retirement and trying to attain good health in two weeks because you want to go on your big holiday. You have to plan for retirement with your money and you have to plan for retirement with your health.'

Here are some thoughts on the ultimate investment, based on the advice of health and nutrition professionals. Like me you may find you can't always stick to it, but try to follow these guidelines most of the time.

Diet

If we are what we eat, then what are we going to be when we turn 64? I'm looking around at some of my peers and I'm wondering what kind of life they'll have in retirement. In fact, I worry: all this money, all these assets, so much work to get there, and for what? A bad back? Diabetes? Heart disease?

Even if you can't be bothered getting to the gym or going for a run or a walk, diet is the one thing that every person can do to make themselves healthier and happier as they age. It's simply what you eat. If you can't be disciplined about this, what can you be disciplined about?

My first suggestion to anyone who values the idea of being healthy in retirement is to seek out a professional—either a doctor with a whole-of-life approach to your health, or a dietician—and get a diet tailored for who you are, how you live and where you want to go. If they identify problems with how you're eating and drinking, listen to them and try to fit their advice into the goal–strategy–discipline system. Usually they'll write it down—then it's up to you. You have to follow through.

I believe that diet is one of the fastest ways that anyone can turn around their health. With a good diet you not only immediately start functioning better, but your mental performance improves too. If you're putting crap into your body, you're going to be getting crap results both at a body and a brain level.

Dr Jennifer Hunter, a GP who also believes in some alternative medicines, tells me that many cases of depression may not be *caused* by diet per se, but are certainly linked to diet and helped along by it. So are many diseases and conditions: she says adult-onset diabetes, cancer, heart disease, arthritis and many of the organ-failure diseases are either directly caused by or related to what we eat and drink. Diet can affect their likelihood, their onset and how quickly you can beat them back.

The doctors I speak to tell me that diet is not a one-size-fits-all solution. I recommend that you speak with a professional and take note of their assessment. And then you have to show discipline and make a concerted attempt to follow through. This is an investment in yourself. We know all the dangers. It's time to make the investment.

Exercise

I'm a very lucky person. I grew up in a family where my parents thought that a good diet and a lot of exercise were the basics of a healthy life. They still do. So I grew up playing lots of sport, doing lots of running and playing and climbing.

However, I didn't exactly find it easy to start a routine of exercise again as an adult. The unaccustomed discipline was as hard for me as for anyone. Once you're into one routine for work, it's very hard to fit another completely different routine in there as well. But you have to find a way—that's what discipline is. And here's the other lesson: whether it's work or stress or bad thoughts or drinking, it's all a habit. So you can create good habits too. And once you've brought out all that discipline to get yourself going, it becomes easier because it's becoming a habit. We're creatures of habit—good and bad.

Let's run through the benefits of regular exercise as constantly lectured to me by my medical friends:

- It builds muscle, which gives you strength.
- It makes you use your heart and lungs and thus keeps them healthy.
- It makes your blood pump around the body, taking nutrients where they don't usually go and picking up toxins.
- It burns calories, thus aiding in weight loss.
- It raises your metabolic rate, creating a genuine and healthy appetite.
- It helps you sleep better.
- It releases brain chemicals called endorphins which make you feel good and smooth out your moods.
- It reduces the likelihood of diseases such as heart disease, some cancers, osteoporosis, hypertension, adult-onset diabetes and even depression.

- It boosts the immune system.
- It lowers blood pressure.
- It increases the 'good' cholesterol.
- It promotes the correct blood-sugar levels.
- If you do it enough, you build stamina—the strength to go on and a natural boost to your everyday confidence.

So if exercising on a regular basis is so good for us, why are we so bad at it? In the United States, the adult population is 70 per cent sedentary—that is, they sit too long, don't exercise, don't walk anywhere, don't play with their kids or walk the dog. Australia is going the same way. There are scientific estimates that a sedentary lifestyle after a certain age poses as much of a risk of stroke or heart disease as smoking does. Your lungs aren't blowing, your heart isn't pumping, your arteries are clogging up and your brain is functioning well below what it should. All of this because you want to watch TV rather than look after your body.

The Report of the NSW Chief Health Officer (2006) had a very interesting statistic: 57 per cent of adult men and 42 per cent of adult women were obese in 2005. I say this is interesting because there's one main set of circumstances that creates obesity, and that's too much of the wrong food combined with too little exercise. It's that simple—it's about the easiest formula you'll ever read when it comes to investing. Yet in Australia's biggest state, half of its adult population is obese.

Exercise is up there with diet as one of those things you can start doing today to reverse the onset of all sorts of preconditions to certain diseases. If you know that diet and exercise can do this, and can do it in a lasting way, then you're going to have to come up with a plan for establishing some good habits prior to your retirement. You have to get your mix of assets and their weightings right in order to ensure that you have the right amount of money when you retire, and you have to get your exercise patterns right before you get to retirement. And patterns are what they'll have to be; exercise is only any good if it's regular. You do it irregularly and that's when you pull muscles and injure yourself. You do it regularly and you build stamina, you build a healthy heart and lungs and strong muscles.

The more I speak with doctors and trainers and sports science people about this, the more I realise that any amount of exercise is beneficial to any person. Your age, race, body shape, gender, socioeconomic standing or profession are irrelevant. Exercise is always better than no exercise, and a habit of exercise will take you further and further away from being in the danger zone of many diseases.

Mind

Have you noticed one of the big stories of this decade? It's the numbers of highly educated, highly paid people who are having to take stress leave and extended leave of absence from their jobs because they're stressed, depressed, burned out or burdened with chronic fatigue. People are walking away from careers, they're hitting the bottle, they're destroying marriages, alienating their children and limping towards retirement with some terrible baggage.

Mental illness—an unhealthy mind—has become a big problem in Australia. And the advances in its prevalence seem to have coincided with the ageing of the baby boomers.

Brain disorders pose the highest cost—both economic and in terms of social capital—to Australia of any disease group, accounting for over 22 per cent of the expense, double that of cancer (11.3%). Brain disorders are predicted to contribute a progressively higher percentage of the burden of disease in Australia, so that by the year 2020 they will comprise 27 per cent of the healthcare bill. About 2.6 million adult Australians suffer from at least one mental illness episode per year, and according to the Australian Institute of Health and Welfare, around one in six Australian men suffer from depression.

I can't think of any greater waste of time than working like a maniac for all those years, for all that money and all that security, so you can get to retirement as a burned-out, depressed wreck. Why are we doing it to ourselves?

As I said above, around the age of 30 I committed myself to adopting systems and techniques to manage my way around this trap of overworking, becoming isolated from what was important, and falling into a well of unhappiness. My concept then—as it is now—was that if I could train my body to be healthy with a disciplined strategy of diet and exercise then I could do the same with my mind. I didn't think I could become Einstein, but I felt that diet and exercise, along with some techniques and some discipline to follow them through, was something that would keep my mind ticking along in not only a productive fashion but with some happiness too.

Much of the depression and anxiety we bring on ourselves comes from work stress. I know there are young people who don't work who are depressed, but I'm talking about working adults—people who are planning for retirement, who are thinking about their super and trying to get the mortgage paid down while probably also raising kids.

We see this in our workplaces. We see the people who are not coping, who are getting more manic and then more sad and withdrawn. They're often men; women seem to be able to express their anxiety better and that creates a safety valve. Men soldier on, and what happens to them as retirees is nothing but trouble. It's interesting to note from Ron Penny that of the nine major causes of heart disease, one of them is stress (others are lack of exercise, insufficient fruit and veggie intake, and so on).

I don't discount any of the physiological reasons for an unhealthy mind. But I suspect many problems come back to stress, time management and personal care. Diet and exercise help in the first instance. They make people happier. However, I think people should seek medical help if they're in trouble and they know it. You already know the type of doctor I'd seek out—someone with a whole-of-life approach who could see me in terms of everything I am and do, rather than just a symptom who needs drugs. But for people who are wanting to stay happy and mentally healthy, following are some of the tips I use myself and that I have picked up from my professional advisers. These tips work best after you've changed to a good diet and are doing some form of exercise. I now know from Dr Hunter that when patients present with stress and depression problems, the first thing a doctor looks at is diet and exercise.

- **Space:** Allow at least five minutes between each work meeting and use this time to be very quiet and to clear your mind.
- **Full stop:** I believe that stress levels peak and become unhealthy when you take your work, anxiety and worries back home. Have a ritual end to your day, something that signals that you have finished: I have a shower and a glass of wine. That's it—that's the end of my working day.
- **Worry box:** Even if you refuse to bring work home with you, you still bring the anxiety about what's going to happen tomorrow or what you did wrong today. I use the worry box: it's a wooden box on a tallboy in my house. Before I have a shower at the end of the day I consciously take the anxiety—the thing that's niggling at me, the thing I'm annoyed about—out of my head and place it in the worry box. That's where the worry stays and it can't come out. You have to train yourself to do this properly, and you have to be serious about it. But with practice it does work.

- **Read:** I recommend that you read a magazine or book for pleasure once a day at least, even if it's only for a few minutes. It's your brain—you have to let it relax and enjoy itself from time to time.
- **Acceptance:** If you can accept that human existence itself is sometimes stressful, rather than deny it or try to be entirely free of it, then I think you start from a much better position.
- **Meditate:** If you can practise meditation or just really good breathing and relaxation techniques, you can use these in all sorts of situations that you may not have imagined. Even a small respite for your brain each day is better than none at all.

Stress is something we have to watch if we want to be healthy in retirement. Dr Hunter tells me that failing to manage stress not only damages the mind, but also puts stresses on the body. As she explains it:

> If you're not managing stress you can actually stress the brain with too many negative thoughts and emotions. You can overstress your body because your stress levels are hitting your nerves, your immune system, your hormonal system, your adrenal glands, which start working too hard and ends in burn-out and depression. Or, you attempt to march on with no satisfaction in your work, to an early retirement.
>
> It's sad to watch and it can absolutely be managed as long as we can get to it early.

One of the things I like about Dr Hunter is that she doesn't make me sound so harsh about life being all about stress. She agrees:

> Health is not a static state of perfection, and neither is life. Without adversity, it's not life. So it's about coping and finding the techniques that work best for you. I tell patients that a child has to get a few colds to build its immunity to worse colds in the future. It doesn't mean the child never gets a cold again. It's the same in the adult world; we have to accept the bad days with the good; we sometimes have to say 'the milk's already been spilled'.

Happiness

Your soul, I believe, sustains you every bit as much as your diet or your mental capacity. Your soul is an energy source for your own happiness. At the centre of this idea is happiness. And as you can see from the way I explain it, this soulful happiness can only come from within. You can't take it from anyone.

This may sound unfair, but I believe it's true and I also believe that it leads any intelligent person to realise the obvious:

Only I can make me happy.

No-one else can make you happy. It's not their job. Their actions and words can make you unhappy, for sure, but if you're sitting around waiting for a spouse or a boyfriend or a colleague or a parent or a sibling or a child to make you happy, you're going to be waiting a long time.

Others make us smile, they make us laugh, but they can't make us happy.

Only I can make me happy.

This is my belief. Many others believe it too. And once you believe this, you have only two choices: either I'm going to be happy, or I'm going to be unhappy.

I have a basic strategy for this that probably works for others too. Smell the roses. If it's a beautiful day in Sydney, I might walk down to the Domain and feel the breeze on my face for a few minutes. I like the rainforest, so when I'm up the coast on my farm I like to walk out into the forest in the middle of the night and just smell and hear it. That sort of thing fills me up. I like travelling too, with no work commitments. I just like going somewhere for a few days and soaking my surroundings in. I've done this all my life.

It's your investment in yourself. It's your soul and it's your job to keep it topped up. Some people will be reading this and thinking that their problem is their environment, their spouse, their co-workers, their family. I can only reiterate what I said above. Others will always try to make you unhappy, but only you can make you happy.

You can't control the people who want to make you unhappy. So you'll have to control your own happiness. This is where it becomes a management issue in the goal–strategy–discipline sense. You can set the goal, you have the strategy and you have to find the discipline from somewhere.

You have to do this all your life and only you can do it.

The next generation

If you have children, two big concerns are: Will I do a good enough job of my own finances to not put a burden on them in my old age? And have I taught them enough about the important things in life so that they'll be successful in their own right?

There's no easy answer to these questions. We all have to do what we feel is right and best.

The first issue is what this book is about: setting yourself up sufficiently so that you won't be a financial burden on your kids. You can do this by stating your goals, developing a strategy and maintaining discipline. Then you focus on your property, shares, superannuation and your own well-being. These four investments are the basic building blocks of security, wealth and happiness in the second half of your life. If you manage these things properly, there's going to be a long time to deal with your kids, because with life expectancies going into the eighties for both men and women at the moment, there will be 25 years of retirement for most people. That's a quarter of a century; that's two generations; that's the length of the average mortgage.

My advice about this is that not only should you not be a drain on your kids financially—or in terms of health issues—but it would be nice to be in such a situation that you could help them out with money. You don't have to give your adult kids actual cash—you can use your unencumbered properties as security for their property purchases. You can work in their business for low or no wages. You can mind their kids, you can lend them money to start a business, you can shout them a holiday. The point of the exercise is that you want to be in a situation at retirement where you have enough income that you can keep giving to your kids—if you wish—as well as yourself. The fundamentals of this have been covered: we need to use our income-earning years to buy assets that will create income when we no longer work. We need an unencumbered house, a portfolio of shares and a superannuation fund that we've added extra to over the years, over and above the 9 per cent Superannuation Guarantee.

If you're lucky, they'll look after you when you're infirm and need their help.

The asset-building side of things is only one part. Income and asset protection are equally important. I've spoken about this at length in the previous chapter. But it's the kids who this is so often about. Things like wills, life insurance, income protection insurance, powers of attorney and even funeral bonds won't get you any prizes for being the coolest parent in the world. But any one of these things will be a huge bonus for the kids if anything ever happens to you. So both your own efforts to build wealth and your attempts to protect it are helping the children in their future.

The second point is a bit trickier: how to prepare a child for their own financial journey.

Teaching your kids about money

I think the first place to start is to acknowledge that when you talk with your kids about all the important things it's ridiculous to ignore one of the main aspects of anyone's life: and that is the earning, the spending, the investing and the growing of money.

I grew up in a time when no-one's parents spoke about money. It was like a secret. Not just in my house, but in all of my friends' houses. In those days, kids didn't know what houses cost, they didn't know what adults earned, they had no idea about investing. It was none of our business.

Now, things are different. Children are raised to understand that there are no jobs for life, that the government is not going to do everything for them. And in this environment, money becomes more of their business. They see business stories on the front pages of newspapers, business stories lead the news bulletins on TV, and stories like the collapse of HIH and One.Tel have an impact even in the child's mind: if your footy club can't get its accident insurance cover for the players, then you may only be ten years old but the subject of money is having an impact on you.

So these things are now part of everyday discourse, and everyday discourse includes our kids. Yet the kids are still kids. Have you ever seen parents trying to get twelve-year-olds to fill out those budget planners that you're supposed to go through with your children? They can't concentrate on these for more than a few seconds. They don't care—you have no chance. Kids have their DNA set to filter out anything a parent says to them. It's just 'return to sender'.

And this is especially so when you talk about the joys of saving. Kids learn by you *showing*, not *telling*.

So what do they know about savings that you've shown them lately? Parents don't save, so their kids don't save. It's clear—we're net borrowers rather than net savers. Yet kids get these finance 'activity packs' foisted on them with all these budget planners and savings spreadsheets and even dummy investment portfolios. Actually, most kids are quite aware that a savings account will take more from them in fees than they'll earn in interest. That's about the end of that.

Yet, at the same time, you can't spoil your kids. What's the point of just handing over money every time they demand it? We all know where that leads to: kids demanding more and more and more. This is irresponsible, even though it's easier for us to just hand over the $10 or the $20 every time the child wants it.

The harder thing is to confront the issue and try to deal with it. The child needs money—you want them to have respect for the stuff.

I think the best that parents can do when educating their kids about money is to teach by example and strike a balance between allowing kids to enjoy their childhoods and showing them the basics.

How to strike this balance without becoming too technical or too moralistic about money? That's the hard part. And honestly, I think most parents already know where to draw the line. A child deserves a hassle-free existence while they're still young, but you do them no favours by sending them into the world with no idea of how to handle a credit card or a bank account.

My system

As I said, I'm the father of four sons, three of them still in their teens. For the last two years I've been following a system I invented myself. I didn't invent it because I'm a child-raising genius; I did it my way because I couldn't find a system for our times that allowed kids to be kids while still making them grasp the value of money and the benefits of being organised with it.

I didn't like the idea of pocket money—it didn't make sense. Pocket money is never linked to anything, yet it carries with it this huge sense of entitlement: 'My pocket money is $20 a week, so where is it? I want it *now*!' Cleaning up round the house and making your bed is not something a child should be paid for, is it? Isn't that a child just playing their part in the community that is the home?

I didn't like the constant handing-over of money and neither could I see the point in telling them that they had to do it all on their own. I was somewhere in between this give-away notion of money and the approach that's moralistic and mean. One way tells kids that there's no value in money; the other trains them to resent work and perhaps even fear money, since earning it is associated with having to work when your friends are having fun.

My own system seems to be working thus far. This is how I did it.

When I realised that a previous money scheme was not working for the boys I decided to test them with the kind of approach you'd get in any corporation or government department. I decided to make each of the boys write a submission which would list their expenses and needs for each week, and what their budget would therefore be.

The background to this had been a disastrous period of money just being handed over willy-nilly, which had turned too often into those fights that all parents know about: someone else got $20, so why can't they have $20? And on and on and on . . .

It was stressing me out, and I wondered how parents who use this technique actually handle the harassment. I couldn't stand it. Our new system would cover all of that by requiring the boys to make an honest attempt to list their weekly expenses and charge me for it.

I was actually pleasantly surprised at the accuracy and the thought that went into the submissions. They were detailed, they seemed fair, and rather than overestimate their costs in some cases they underestimated. Even my youngest—who was twelve when he did his first submission—got up to speed very quickly after he'd left some obvious costs off his submission; when I pointed this out to him, he came back very quickly with a revised submission.

The final lists for each boy—the oldest was eighteen—were comprehensive catalogues of what high school kids need. In their budgets were daily school lunches, school breakfasts, bus money (and petrol money for the eldest of them, who drives a car), mobile phone recharge costs (prepaid, of course), clothes money, weekend money and what have you. Everything they needed in any week had to be there in writing, and they understood that what they received each week was going to be it.

I reviewed each of these submissions, argued for some points, increased their estimates on others, and made them come back with the final versions. We signed off on each one and then the system began.

Part of the arrangement was that each of the boys was going to be paid their money into a bank account each Friday. The money would turn up in their bank accounts on the Monday and they would have to eke that out until the next Monday. Sometimes they run out of money because there's a one-off run of expenses, but they have to come to me and argue it. They know I don't want the hassle of them demanding more money, so these requests have been very few.

I wanted a system that ran smoothly and took the pressure off both me and the kids. There are plenty of opportunities in life for adults to argue about money—I didn't want to do it with my kids ten times a day.

But along with a smoother payment system for the boys came some added bonuses in the form of learning.

- Because I didn't preach and moralise, it took the emotion out of the issue and got them focused on what they needed and how they were going to justify it to me. Sounds like a budget.
- The single weekly payments very quickly disciplined the boys into aligning their spending with their income. One of them even cut his spending for a few

weeks and bought an iPod. Sounds like cash flow management.

- The boys seemed to come to the realisation quickly that this money was a useful and valuable asset, and that if they were careful with how they spent it they'd end up with a surplus they could spend on themselves. It sounds like 'money doesn't grow on trees', but no-one had to say it.
- I didn't set a template for this system—I made them tell me. This has made them not only disciplined about where money goes, but it has made them focused on where it comes from.
- I know how much money they get a week and basically I know where it goes. I'm not as exposed to my kids getting into the bad stuff, because basically they don't have the discretionary spending for it.
- They're not only learning how banks work, they've gained more respect for the security of their money. They've all lost their wallets at some point, and they now understand that having a PIN that is unique and that only you know is important.
- Having to account for weekly expenses makes them understand inflation. It's been almost two years since we started this, and they've applied for two increases because of rising bus fares and petrol. They understand the shrinking value of money over time, without me having to tell them a thing about it.
- The biggest thing, and the biggest surprise: my boys like the responsibility, they like the discipline and they

like the freedom they get out of having to run their own finances.

A few tips if you're thinking of doing this system with your own kids. First, I don't call it an 'allowance'. I got that straight with them from the start. I said 'this is the money you get', and so ever since then our system has been called The Money You Get. My reasoning for this was that when you call something an allowance, or pocket money, you turn something that is a privilege into a right. And kids are already so surrounded by a sense of entitlement that making money they are *given* a part of that entitlement just didn't seem to work.

Second, I would emphasise that you have to put the onus on the kids to come to you with the submission; they have to put it in writing and they have to be prepared to discuss it without being demanding and bratty. I think this is an important step because it means you're making them take a responsible step: they have to calculate their expenses, they have to add them up, and they then have to make their money cover those expenses each week. They also get to wear the responsibility for getting it wrong. And if they get it wrong, they have to come back with a revised submission for The Money You Get.

Third, the big thing they take from this is discipline. And the reason they learn without even being taught is that you never said a word about it. Remember, a child thinks the most natural thing in the world is to ignore a parent when the parent is lecturing.

I should expand on the last point. I often get asked to speak with kids about money habits and the importance of buying property and so on. Invariably kids have to be told that hard work and discipline are what make people successful. But this is not something a teenager can hear.

Discipline is one thing—they're surrounded by that at school and at home. And I reckon that if they get too much of that external discipline, they become compliant young adults. And compliant young adults just go along with whatever is around them, and that can mean the bad stuff.

But it's self-discipline that they really need, and that's something they'll usually have to learn by making mistakes. We don't want them to make huge mistakes on their own—so we try to put trainer wheels on them. A parent says things like 'in my day' and they just tune out. And that's one of the reasons I'm happy about The Money You Get system. You don't have to lecture them, because they have to make it work themselves, and they make their own mistakes along the way. And therefore they're learning from their own mistakes, which is the most powerful teacher for anyone.

I'm not opposed to teaching kids about the joys of saving, the importance of getting your first home and the value of investing in shares. But is that what you tell them in their teens? Or can that wait until they're earning their own money in their first job? I'm not sure that any of these things is going to mean a lot to a person unless they've been earning for at least a couple of years and have got a feel for what money they can earn and where they might like to put it.

The final thing I would say about kids and finances is that everyone has a slightly different approach and mine is on the helpful side. As long as my boys are working hard and doing their best to save and buy a house, they can count on my support for the deposit or the stamp duty. When it comes to money I think parenting and being a child is a two-way thing: the parents want to see that there's some effort, that there's a sense of value attached to something like a house purchase. We don't want to raise brats. But neither do we want our own money and savings to be for naught. If I have the money, I help my kids reach their goals. It's that simple. We're family—we help and support one another. I don't understand the 'do it on your own' approach with kids. If the kids get to an age where they know you can afford to help—but you won't—it will breed resentment. How are you supposed to tell a child about the value of property or shares when you're deliberately not helping them? What are you teaching them—that you're mean? That money is something used to punish them?

If the goal is to have the kids learn to do things under their own steam, then you can create a reward system rather than a punishment: make it a matching offer where you match them dollar for dollar in their race to get a deposit, or whatever it is you can afford.

If you link money and investing with punishing your kids, you may not like the results. Make money the reward and, like my payment system for the boys, the kids will come around of their own will.

Raising healthy and happy children

The ultimate investment is ensuring you provide the building blocks for your children to lead happy and healthy lives. The reason it's the ultimate investment is that we're raising the next generation, and they're raising the next generation after that. Imagine if this line of your family had the habits and the skills, the diet and the lifestyle to lead happy and healthy lives? And they passed these values and habits on to their kids, and so on, and so on? If everyone did this, we'd have a much happier and healthier society, and one in which things like childhood diabetes and pre-adolescent obesity were unheard of.

One of the sobering things that has happened in my lifetime has been the rise of the wealthy unwell; that is, people with incredible wealth when viewed on a global scale who use this wealth and luxury to feed themselves to death. The scourge of sugar-loaded, salt-laden processed foods, together with childhood pastimes such as TV, video games, the internet and messaging, has created youngsters with physical shapes that just weren't around when I was young. When I was at primary school, a ten-year-old kid with an obesity problem was a rarity and they invariably had some sort of hormonal imbalance. Now, when you look at groups of schoolkids going by, it looks like half the class is obese. Are they being made to do sport? Are their diets monitored? Are they having health checks?

Ron Penny now tells me that the leading public health experts are warning that Australia is currently at a 'tipping point'. We could be embarking, right now, on a phase in our history which will see the kids currently aged fifteen years and younger becoming the first generation in our nation's history to have a shorter life expectancy than the generation before them. The figures show the situation getting worse, so the kids currently aged six and younger will have shorter life expectancies than the kids in their late teens.

And guess what? We did it to them.

Making sure we raise healthy and happy children and grandchildren may well be the ultimate investment. But how do we do it? Here are some observations.

Diet

It all starts with diet. Most experts agree that the main culprits behind poor diet in children are too much sugar, salt, fat and trans-fats, which can in turn lead to health problems such as diabetes and obesity.

I advise any parent wanting to make the ultimate investment to take their child to see their GP. Kids can have check-ups too. Check-ups can catch things that casual observation can't. And they can create a personalised diet and follow-up regime for the child. They might even get you—the parent—to start a diet diary and actually log what the child is eating. Diet diaries are revelatory in their own right and can be a wake-up call to parents.

The alternatives to bad foods are simple: all of the sugar that a young body craves exists in fruit and some vegetables.

The trick, as always, is to make sure that plenty of fresh fruit and whole foods are always available. As the child gets older, we come back to showing rather than telling. If you eat an apple as a snack, your kids are going to think that's normal. If you eat vegetables and salads with your meals, the kids will too.

But unless you eat these foods, all the lecturing in the world is going to have zero effect.

Exercise

There's not much to say here because we already know it. Kids need exercise, and they need a lot of it. If adults need 30 minutes a day of cardio exercise—panting, sweating, exerting—then children need an hour. Where are they going to find that hour? As Ron Penny said to me, 'Turn off the PlayStation; turn off the TV—they'll find the hour, believe me.' I couldn't agree more.

In the NSW Chief Health Officer's Report (2006), the finding was that one-quarter of NSW schoolchildren are not getting enough exercise each day. Why not? Our job, as people making the ultimate investment, is to be leaders rather than followers in this regard. If we grab a soccer ball and go out into the park, the kids will follow. If we grab the tennis racquets and make for the courts or announce that we're going to the swimming pool, then that's what's happening. We are the parents—we are the leaders. You don't have to throw the PlayStation out the window, but everything has to happen in moderation. If a child's health and happiness is suffering because he's glued to an Xbox, guess who has to show leadership on that front?

Worried that you'll lose popularity with the child? Tough! Parenting isn't a popularity contest—it's about showing wisdom and giving love. And when I say 'love', I don't mean the kind that's easy for the parents, the kind where you say 'yes' to every request. Sometimes parental love is doing the things that are hard on kids and on parents.

Yes, sometimes it's more convenient to have a child locked away playing video games, but maybe what they really need is some leadership. As in all things with kids, I suggest showing rather than telling. If a child sees you going out for a jog or playing regular tennis or going to the gym, then that is a more powerful piece of leadership than simply lecturing.

However you do it, the ultimate investment is going to involve you developing an exercise habit for your kids.

Happiness

Our kids need us for two reasons when it comes to their happiness. They need us to love and reassure them as they're growing up, and they need to be shown how to do it for themselves as they develop into adults.

This is mildly controversial: I know there are lots of people who argue that some kids are allowed to be depressed and angry and antisocial and their parents can't do anything about it. At this point you have to decide who you are: personally, I think happiness can be learned as a skill and developed and practised and perfected over a lifetime. I don't buy this idea that some kids have an excuse to drop by the wayside. I don't think you help them by telling them they can behave any way they want.

The point I made in a previous chapter about life never being stress free also applies to our kids. Every day of their lives they're going to find things that are new, that they can't master straightaway, and that will leave them feeling unhappy about the way something turned out. We don't help the child by telling them that the challenge itself was the bad idea; we give them more skills for developing their own happiness by encouraging them not to give up, by reminding them that there's always another day, that it's not the end of the world. This is where love and reassurance has to become a daily habit: you can't control what happens to them at school or with their mates or on the sports field. But you can get them in the habit of loving themselves and looking after and nurturing that part of them that some people call the soul and others call the spirit.

In the end we all want our kids to be healthy and happy. But we have to be honest with ourselves about it. If a child is obese, what are you doing about it? If a child can't walk up a flight of stairs without being out of breath, what's your response? If a child has no confidence, what's your involvement with that?

Getting our kids into the right habits is the ultimate investment. It's the most important thing of all, but that often makes it the hardest.

CONCLUSION: ACHIEVING FINANCIAL SECURITY

I started this book talking about the two great dreams that form the bookends of many Australians' financial focus: owning their home and having a comfortable retirement.

Your own home not only gives you a place to live, but also an appreciating asset and one you can use to borrow money and create wealth. And Australians are good at housing. It's part of our psyche to save enough money to buy a house and get a mortgage. Then we take years to pay it off and only in dire circumstances do we consider selling it and moving into the rental market.

It's a bit different when it comes to saving for a comfortable retirement. For some, the comfortable retirement is the reward for all the hard work—the scrimping and saving to buy the house, the superannuation contributions, the share portfolio and maybe the investment home. But for many, the comfortable retirement, at least in a financial sense, never eventuates.

The government knows it and has spent the last two decades trying to encourage people to save more for retirement, through the introduction of the Superannuation Guarantee and tax changes that have made saving for retirement more attractive. But the problem will only grow bigger.

The baby boomers will soon start to retire, and the number of people working as a proportion of the number of people retired will halve. That means the working population's ability to pay for age pensions through the tax system will be severely diminished. The bottom line is simple: whether you are 20, 40 or 60 years old, you have to take saving for retirement seriously and you have to develop goals, create a strategy and have the discipline to follow it.

Goals, strategy and discipline are three of the most often repeated words in this book, because that's what saving for retirement is about. It's how I try to live my life, not just in terms of investing and superannuation but also in my property development business and my efforts to remain healthy so I can enjoy my twilight years.

As I mentioned in the introduction, you should know where you're trying to get to, know how it's going to be achieved, and be confident that you have what it takes to follow through.

I started my own journey into the retirement savings world at 49 years of age. I realise now that I should have started when I was 25. But I also realise it's never too late to start. A 60-year-old who has never thought about super will have a more comfortable retirement in five years if they start thinking about their financial future now.

Along the way I took time to understand things that were important to my financial future. These were the Key Concepts: income, risk, diversification and market sentiment. I began to better understand the pros and cons of investing in shares, and the benefits of high-yielding stocks.

I've understood property and the need to own it for a long time, but over the last few years I've learnt plenty about the need for superannuation. And I've learnt that ideally your retirement savings plan will include your own share portfolio and an investment property. As important as any of that, I know that your health and wellbeing will, every bit as much as your financial position, dictate your happiness in retirement.

I've been lucky in my business career and made some money. But I only got there through hard work and sticking to my three-pronged formula: goals, strategy, discipline. It certainly didn't happen overnight. Investing my money now, I still stick to that formula.

I hope this book gives you a few insights into investing and saving for retirement. Some of the tips are usually reserved for the truly wealthy, but there's no reason everyone can't adopt them. Understand your personal retirement strategy and take charge of it. No-one else will. And remember that if you can own your own home, grow your superannuation fund, build up a share portfolio and, with a bit of luck, afford an investment property, you are well on the way to financial security.

GLOSSARY

Absolute return funds Managed funds, or hedge funds, that target 'absolute returns' aim to produce positive returns in both rising and falling markets. Such funds typically have greater scope to use sophisticated trading strategies.

Allocated pension A person's retirement savings is invested and regular payments are received from that investment; it has tax advantages and provides a regular income in retirement years.

Alternative investments As the name suggests, investments outside mainstream asset classes are called alternative investments and include hedge funds, private equity and derivatives. They tend to suit individuals with higher risk profiles. The one common element is that managers of alternative investments seek to provide consistent, positive annual returns.

Annuity Purchased from life insurance companies to provide a regular income (generally) for a maximum of 25 years. They're usually adjusted for inflation.

Asset classes The categories of investments people can put their money into. Common asset classes include cash, fixed interest, property and shares.

Australian Prudential Regulation Authority (APRA) A federal government institution that regulates the financial services industry and oversees banks, credit unions, building societies, general, life and reinsurance companies, and most members of the superannuation industry. Its goal is to ensure a stable, efficient and competitive financial system.

Australian Securities and Investments Commission (ASIC) A federal government institution that regulates and enforces company and financial services laws to protect consumers, investors and creditors. It aims to promote confident and informed participation by investors and consumers in the financial system.

Benchmark returns A measure of the total performance of an asset class, such as the S&P/ASX 200 or 90-day bank bills.

Blue chip Top quality companies on the Australian Stock Exchange with large market capitalisations and a strong track record.

Cash Highly stable and low-returning investment. Cash is short-term, market-traded financial instruments generally accessed by investors through cash management trusts. The capital is quite secure, but cash can make a poor investment because after tax and inflation you may earn a negative return.

Cash flow The money you have available to pay one-off and recurring expenses. For businesses and individuals alike, cash flow is crucial to being able to operate or live; for an individual it includes everything from money for food to school fees, holidays and investments.

Co-contribution If you earn income and make extra after-tax contributions into your superannuation account, the government will pay a co-contribution into your account. Rules apply—you need to earn less than $58,980 and the amount of the co-contribution depends on your income and the amount you contribute.

Defined-benefit fund The amount you receive on retirement is defined by a set formula, normally reflecting length of service. Defined-benefit funds were common in the public service, but are generally now closed to new participants.

Defined-contribution fund The minimum amount you can contribute to your superannuation fund is defined (or legislated), but your final payout on retirement depends on your level of contributions and investment earnings less expenses. Also known as an accumulation fund.

Derivatives Financial instruments whose value comes from something else. Essentially they are arrangements between investors who want to buy or sell assets, such as shares, sometime in the future but want to organise the deal immediately. Common derivative contracts in financial markets include futures, forwards, options and swaps.

Diversification Ensuring there is a good mix of asset classes in your investment portfolio, and a good mix of investments within the asset classes.

Dividend A payment to shareholders of a company, normally taken from the profits of that company. A franked dividend carries a tax credit which can be offset against a shareholder's tax liability. If the company pays the full company tax rate, the dividends are 'fully franked' (see **Franking credits**).

Equity The part of an asset that you own. You can have equity in a house or in a company (see **Shares**).

Fixed interest Interest paid on an investment, at a predetermined rate, over a set period of time. In Australia, fixed-interest investments are typically investments in bonds (which is an 'IOU') issued by the federal or state governments or a large company. The issuers pay regular interest payments and, when the bond matures, they repay the principal plus any interest owing.

Franking credits Franking credits in Australia (also known as imputation credits) were introduced in 1987 to stop double taxing of company earnings. Companies that pay tax on their earnings can distribute 'fully franked' or 'partly franked' dividends to shareholders. The idea is that the company has already paid tax on the money that is used to pay dividends, so the shareholder shouldn't have to also pay tax. The shareholder receives an imputation credit which they can use to lower their tax bill. (See **Dividends**.)

Fund manager A commercial organisation that pools and manages investors' money for a fee. A managed fund is an investment vehicle that is professionally managed. In Australia, managed funds are commonly used to gain exposure to different types of asset classes, including fixed interest, local and international shares, and alternative investments.

Gearing Occurs when you borrow money to invest in growth assets. When the income received from your investment is less than the interest you pay, it is called negative gearing.

Growth investor An investor looking for long-term increases in the value of their investments, usually in shares. Growth investors look for companies with fast-growing sales and revenue, strong management and a sound business strategy.

Hedge fund Although difficult to define, broadly a hedge fund manager uses gearing and derivatives to achieve returns. Hedge funds are often characterised by an absolute return philosophy (as opposed to a benchmark return).

Hedging Taking an action that alleviates risk. Hedging is similar to taking out insurance against adverse movements in the value of an investment.

Index fund A fund manager attempts to replicate the performance of a benchmark index. Index investing in the Australian share market generally means trying to replicate the performance of the S&P/ASX 200 or All Ordinaries Index.

Instalment warrant The holder of an instalment warrant is entitled to buy a share, at a stipulated price, over a set period, by making an additional future payment. Instalment warrants can have tax advantages and may allow the holder to receive dividends.

Investments In superannuation and personal investing, investments generally fall into five categories: cash, fixed interest, property, shares, and alternative investments (see elsewhere in Glossary).

Large cap Refers to the largest companies listed on the Australian Stock Exchange. Broadly they are the 100 companies with the largest market value.

Listed company See **Share market**.

Marginal tax rate A person's marginal tax rate is the rate of tax on the highest dollar of income you earn in a tax year. The lowest marginal tax rate is 15 per cent and kicks in when an individual earns more than $6000. The top marginal tax rate is 45 per cent and is applied on income over $150,000.

Market capitalisation The total value of a company listed on the Australian Stock Exchange (or other exchange) is its market capitalisation. You can work out the market capitalisation of a company by multiplying the number of shares issued by the share price.

Master trust A vehicle that allows investors, including superannuation funds, to put money into one or more investments through a trust structure. Normally these investments are pools of money managed by a professional fund manager. A discretionary master trust allows an individual investor to select an underlying investment product from a list drawn up by the master trust manager. In a fund of funds, the investor selects a risk profile and the master trust manager matches the profile with the underlying investments.

Mid cap Refers to companies listed on the Australian Stock Exchange with a mid-sized market capitalisation. There is no strict definition, but broadly companies ranked between 100 and 200 in terms of capitalisation are considered mid-cap companies.

Option The right, but not the obligation, to buy or sell a share (or some other asset) at a set price within a set period to retail investors.

Product disclosure statement (PDS) All issuers of financial products must provide a product disclosure statement. It provides information about the issuer, benefits and risks of a certain product, fees and costs, and other information.

Property Investment property comprises retail, commercial, industrial, and tourism and leisure. Investors look to achieve high levels of dependable income and long-term growth in the value of the property.

Property trust An investment in which investors pool their money together to invest in residential or commercial properties. It may be listed or unlisted.

Reserve Bank of Australia An independent federal government institution responsible for monetary policy (e.g. interest rates) in Australia, financial system stability and promoting safety and efficiency in the payments system. Its overriding goal is to achieve low and stable inflation over the medium term, and full employment.

Risk profiling A technique used to determine how much risk an investor is comfortable with. Most risk profiling categorises investors into one of five classes: risk averse, conservative, balanced, growth or aggressive (see Chapter 2).

Salary sacrifice In terms of superannuation, it refers to putting more than the 9 per cent employer contribution of your salary into your super fund. Money that is salary sacrificed is taxed at just 15 per cent, lower than most people's marginal tax rate.

Share market (or stock market) A market which brings together buyers and sellers of shares in a company, some fixed-interest securities and some types of derivatives. Price is determined by the forces of supply and demand. Companies that can be bought and sold on the share market are known as 'listed companies'.

Shares The buyer of a share in a company owns a portion of that company. The investor becomes a shareholder and can reap part of the profit of the company via dividends. Also known as 'equities', shares are the most price volatile asset class, yet can also create the highest returns over the medium and long term and can provide tax-effective income. Ups and downs caused by industry, market or economic fluctuations can spook conservative investors. Some 'defensive' stocks create income with less volatility, but mostly investors are looking for capital growth with this class of asset and are willing to accept the volatility.

Small cap Refers to companies listed on the Australian Stock Exchange with a relatively small market capitalisation. Broadly, these are companies outside the largest 200 companies on the exchange.

Trailing commission A regular payment by a managed fund, generally to a financial planning company in return for promoting and selling the manager's product. It continues for as long as the client remains in the managed fund (even if they no longer use the adviser). The commission is normally a percentage of the amount of money retained in the managed fund.

Trustee A person or legal entity responsible for ensuring that a superannuation or investment fund is properly managed and follows relevant laws.

Value investor An investor who seeks to buy shares in a company when they're cheap and sells them when they're expensive. Most value investors look for companies that are out of favour, or undervalued, in the hope that eventually the market will push the stocks higher.

Wrap account A vehicle which houses an investor's portfolio, often for an annual fee that covers all administrative, commission and management expenses.

REFERENCES

AMP-NATSEM Income and Wealth Report, *Live long and prosper*, AMP, Sydney, 2002.

Australian Prudential Regulation Authority, *Insight: Celebrating 10 years of superannuation data collection 1996–2006*, APRA, Sydney, 2006.

Clare, R., *The Voice of Super*, Association of Superannuation Funds of Australia Resource and Research Centre, Sydney, 2007.

Kelly, S., 'Mapping the behavioural trends of the baby boomers', online presentation to the Committee for Economic Development of Australia (CEDA) 'Demographic Destiny' Conference, Sydney, 23 October 2006.

Lucy, J., *The Financial Advice Industry in Australia, The Regulator's Perspective*, ASIC, Gold Coast, 2006.

MoneyManagement.com, *ACA labels industry as structurally corrupt*, Sydney, 2002.

New South Wales Health, *2006 Health of the People of NSW—Report of the Chief Health Officer,* NSW Department of Health, Sydney, 2006.

Treasury, *Intergenerational Report, 2007*, Commonwealth Government, Canberra, 2007.

USEFUL WEBSITES

www.ybr.com.au
www.wizard.com.au
www.rba.gov.au
www.treasury.gov.au
www.abs.gov.au
www.apra.gov.au
www.understandingmoney.gov.au
www.aph.gov.au/library/pubs/MESI/mesi.pdf
www.asic.gov.au
www.westpacinfo.com.au/RLSCalculator
www.reiaustralia.com.au
www.morningstar.com.au
www.moneymanagement.com.au
www.fido.gov.au/fido/fido.nsf
www.fpa.asn.au/findaplanner

INDEX